BADGES, BAD GUYS & BUSTS

Untold Stories of a DEA Agent

KEITH LEIGHTON

BADGES, BAD GUYS & BUSTS

Untold Stories of a DEA Agent

KEITH LEIGHTON

Badges, Bad Guys & Busts
Untold Stories of a DEA Agent

This is a true story. All of the characters, names, incidents, organizations, and dialogue in this novel are true except for some names that are protected for security purposes.

ISBN: 978-1-7362517-5-1

Library of Congress Control Number: 2021910086

Editor Frank Sabina
Co-editor Erica Meyer Leighton

Cover design by Dana Bree, StoneBear Design
StoneBear Publishing LLC - 05/2021
Milford, PA 18337

www.stonebearpublishing.com

DISCLAIMER

As was repeated to us every day at the DEA Academy, the most important thing to remember in this job is that "Everyone goes home at night." I have always believed that and kept that mantra in the back of my head during operations as an agent and while supervising other agents. With that being said, some of the names and photos in this book have been changed to protect the individuals. However, some real names and photos have been used. In these cases, I received written permission from the individuals involved for this disclosure. In other instances, the individual's real name was used due to the individual being deceased. Additionally, some of the exact investigative techniques have been changed due to the sensitivity of those particular techniques.

ACKNOWLEDGEMENTS

To my parents, Bernie and Marie; my sister Megan, her husband John, and their family, Matthew, Peter, Andrew and Joseph; my beautiful wife, Erica, and our amazing children, Lindsey, Jessica and Casey. Thank you for all the love and support you have given me throughout the years. Although you don't know it, you were the true "heroes" throughout this adventure. I couldn't have done it without you. Thank you

To Peter, Mike and Tom. You know who you are. Thank you for the incredible support that you have always given to me and my family throughout the years. You are true friends.

To Dianne, Earl, Toby, Sam, Charlotte, Skyler, Preston, Austin, Brittany, Ryan and Ava. Thank you for coming into my life and accepting me and my family. You always treated everyone in my family like they were your own and that's an amazing feeling.

To all of my fellow agents, task force officers, DEA administrative staff members, police officers, prosecutors, judges and foreign colleagues. You're the best of the best. None of this could have been done without you. Thank you for many years of friendship, camaraderie and good times. You were the best teammates anyone could have asked for. I owe everything to all of you.

To those that made the ultimate sacrifice while serving this country, you will never be forgotten. You are true American heroes. God bless you all.

A special dedication goes out to my wife, Erica. Although I have had many partners throughout my career with the DEA, you are the best partner I have ever had.

ENDORSEMENTS

"Keith Leighton is one of the most dedicated professionals I've had the honor to work alongside. His ideals and values are incontrovertible as is his belief in service to his country. I am truly blessed to call him a friend."

— **Mauricio Jimenez**
Assistant Special Agent in Charge (retired), Drug Enforcement Administration, 1998-2020

*****

"Keith burst on the scene in Miami as a young, wet-behind-the-ears "Special Agent" ready to change the world. And you know what? He did! I knew from the first time we met that he had every tool required to be a great DEA agent: brains, dedication, integrity and devotion to duty. The most amazing part of Keith's story is that every word is true! Not the movies. Not a made-for-TV drama. Real life--good and bad. Keith made a difference, and frankly is representative of the truly incredible women and men on the front lines of our country's deadly War on Drugs."

— **Guy Lewis**
Director, Executive Office for United States Attorneys, 2002-04
United States Attorney for the Southern District of Florida, 2000-02
Assistant United States Attorney, 1988-2002

*****

"Badges, Bad guys and Busts" is a comprehensive look at the career of one of the finest DEA agents I have ever had the privilege to work with. From cartels to murders... from the wire room to the courtroom, this book has it all".

— **David DeVillers**
Former US Attorney and Assistant US Attorney, Southern District of Oho (2002-2021)

*****

"Keith was one of those agents that was always in the middle of a good case. He was a hard-charger with a sense of humor and understood the power of collaboration in counter-drug law enforcement. Whether he was working multi-ton cocaine transportation cases in Miami, attacking the MDMA surge at the source in Europe or dismantling drug gangs in small-town Ohio, Keith identified the threat and then showed up early each morning and stayed late at night to "make the case." There were many times Keith and I would be sitting together on surveillance or at a bar after a take-down and we'd shake our heads at the audacity of the drug dealers we pursued or marvel at the luck we had catching a break in a tough investigation. Then one of us would say if this were in a book no one would believe it... well believe it! Keith wasn't much of a story-teller or braggart while doing the job so I am glad he got the chance to deliver his story in this fun read about serious crimes now that he's retired. I was fortunate to cross paths with a great crime fighter and patriot like Keith Leighton and dozens others like him. God bless the men and women of the DEA."

— **Richard Bendekovic**,
Drug Enforcement Administration 1991-2016

*****

"Badges, Bad Guys, and Busts gives the reader a rare peek into the exciting career of a Special Agent who did it all! A truly compelling account of the roller coaster ride of personal and professional highs and lows over a long and distinguished career. Honored to be along for part of the ride!"

— **Steve Luzinski**,
Associate Special Agent in Charge, Chicago Field Division
September 1983-May 2010

*****

"One day, during Operation Zorro II, Keith walked into my office with a troubled look on his face and said "boss, we got a problem. The Colombians phone who we are up on, just booked a flight to Vegas to meet up with several other traffickers". I then replied, "Keith, this is not a problem, this is an opportunity. Look at your wiretap order, we can listen to him anywhere in the country. Pack your bags, grab a couple of agents, we are going to Vegas baby". Keith was one those few agents who was meticulous about everything. You always knew when his reports came across your desk, it was well written, well documented and ready for any defense attorney to read and begin to worry how he was going to possibly cross examine this agent on the witness stand."

— **Michael P. McManus,**
Chief of Operations, Mexico & Central America
DEA Headquarters, 2001-2004- retired

*****

"Congratulations to Keith. His book brings back great memories from our time in DEA Miami Field Division/Enforcement Group 9. His investigations and contributions to Group 9 helped keep the reputation of the group solid and resulted in dangerous drugs removed from circulation as well as revenue being denied from high level drug trafficking organizations."

— **Sean Vereault,**
Deputy Chief Inspector, DEA Headquarters
2015-Present

TABLE OF CONTENTS

ABOUT THE AUTHOR

These are true stories by Keith Leighton, retired Drug Enforcement Administration (DEA) Special Agent with 29 years of dedicated service. Born in South Carolina into a career U.S. Air Force family, Keith lived all over the world until his family moved to New Hampshire in 1981. Keith went on to earn a degree from Plymouth State College, Plymouth, NH in 1988 and a master's degree from Springfield College, Springfield, Massachusetts in 1990. Keith signed on with the DEA on November 3, 1991 in the DEA Springfield, MA Resident Office.

After graduating from the DEA Academy in February, 1992, Keith transferred to the DEA Miami Field Division where he served for seven years. He then completed tours in Brussels, Belgium; Providence, Rhode Island; Cincinnati, Ohio and Columbus, Ohio.

He was the recipient of numerous awards and accolades throughout his career in the war on drugs, including two DEA Administrator's Awards, one for Exceptional Service and the other for Group Achievement.

He has two daughters and a step-son and he resides in Columbus, OH with his wife, Erica. These are his stories . . .

Keith Leighton

Introduction

Just as we were about to grab the target to place handcuffs on him, which looked like it was going to be pretty routine since the target was just standing there motionless with his hands up, the target quickly reached into the waistband of his pants and... pulled a gun out, placed it under his chin and blew his head off!! And that was just within my first couple of months....

My name is Keith Leighton. I was hired by the U.S. Drug Enforcement Administration (DEA) in August of 1991. In November of 1991, I started Basic Agent Training in Quantico, Virginia at the FBI Academy as part of Basic Agent Academy Class #87. In February of 1992, I graduated fourth in my class out of 42 students which I was impressed with since I did not have any kind of prior law enforcement experience. Hell, I had never even shot a gun before that. Anyway, I was assigned to the DEA Miami FL Field Division where I spent seven years from 1992 to 1999. I was then assigned to the DEA Brussels, Belgium Country Office from 1999 to 2002 after which I returned to the U.S. where I completed seven more years, 2002 to 2009, assigned to the DEA Providence, RI Resident Office. Following those posts, I accepted a voluntary transfer to the DEA Cincinnati, OH Resident Office and served there from 2009 to 2011 and then accepted an interdivision move to the DEA Columbus, OH District Office starting in 2011. During this time, I was temporarily assigned as a Task Force Agent to the FBI Safe Streets Task Force in Columbus, Ohio from 2013 to 2015. The time came when I decided to retire on June 30, 2020 after 29 years with the DEA. These are my stories.

1
A Dream

Many people ask me how I became a DEA Agent. Or what made me choose this career path. Like most things in life, it was an accident. Well, not an accident, but more of a bunch of random events that sort of all came together. When I went through college and then graduate school, my major in both programs was physical education. Why? Well, like many incoming college freshmen, I didn't have a clue of what I wanted to major in or pursue as a career. I played college football and enjoyed working out so I figured I would just major in physical education. And then when I started grad school, I had to continue in that field. About halfway through grad school, I knew time was running out, and I couldn't go to school the rest of my life.

I remember being home on break and talking to my dad who had retired as a Lieutenant Colonel in the U.S. Air Force after serving for 26 years. He knew that I was unhappy with my major and that I was starting to stress out about what would be the next chapter in my life. He then mentioned law enforcement. He said that he had always noticed how I was always interested in law enforcement throughout my entire life and that maybe I should pursue that. He added that it was his opinion that if I did pursue something like that it should be in federal law enforcement. That was his 26 years of government service speaking right there. No, seriously, he made some very good points. He mentioned that the federal government had the best benefits that you could ever find, in the private or public sector, bar none. The health care, pay, and pension system is unmatched. This is something I can definitely attest to. He also said you never had to worry about getting laid off or let go. Once in a blue moon there is what's called a Reduction in Force (RIF) but the people that are let go are hired back immediately upon the government starting to hire again. Fortunately, I made it 29 years without this ever happening in the DEA. This push for federal law enforcement appealed to me as well because I had always been intrigued by investigations, particularly long-term investigations. It was like one of those 2,000-piece jigsaw puzzles to me. It took one piece at a time over a long period of time. Being an investigator required determination, patience, tenacity, focus on the end result, and a vision. That appealed to me. I remember feeling like a new man after that discussion. I had a dream!! A fresh start. Now I had to figure out how to achieve it.

You need to remember something. This was circa 1989-1990, well before cell phones and the internet. So, I started this crazy journey one day by simply walking into the federal building in Springfield, Massachusetts while I was finishing up graduate school. I literally walked to every federal law enforcement agency office in there and grabbed an application. I went to the DEA, the FBI, the ATF, the U.S. Marshals Service, the U.S. Customs Service, the Border Patrol Agency, the IRS and the U.S. Secret Service. I must be forgetting a few more because I distinctly remember that there were 13 of them in all. Anyway, I was off and running. And I was obsessed. It's all I did in my free time. The majority of these agencies utilize a Standard Form 171 or SF 171 for their job application. And it's **long**! And I was using a typewriter to complete these, as well. Plus, many required recommendations that had to be attached. However, little by little I completed one at a time and sent each out by way of snail mail. Gradually, little by little, I started hearing back from each agency requesting one thing or another and laying out their steps to employment and a timeline.

My life then became as hectic as it had ever been. I was always rushing off to test for something for one of the agencies that I had applied to. It was a panel interview for DEA one day, then a written test for the U.S Marshals Service the next day and then a polygraph exam for the U.S. Secret Service the following day. It went on like this for months. Then the attrition process started. One by one they either started rejecting me, or I decided that the job wasn't for me. For starters, some simply weren't hiring. Others, I just never heard back from. Still others told me I simply didn't qualify. One of these was the FBI which was extremely hard to get into unless you had a law degree, were a CPA, or were fluent in some exotic language like Farsi or Arabic.

As far as deciding that the job wasn't for me, I remember the Border Patrol Agency (now Homeland Security Investigations (HSI)/Immigration and Customs Enforcement (ICE)) offering me a job almost immediately. The one condition was that I would need to relocate to the Southwest Border, become fluent in Spanish once I got there, all for a starting salary of $18,000. That just wasn't for me. I turned them down. One more crossed off the list. As the summer of 1991 approached, I was getting pretty dejected. The only two viable agencies left in the mix were the DEA and the U.S. Secret Service. I was losing hope.

And then, out of the blue, I got a call one day at work. It was a very polite woman who introduced herself and then stated that she was calling from the Drug Enforcement Administration and was calling to offer me a job. I said yes before she could even continue with the particulars. She laughed and asked if I wanted to hear the employment conditions, like the salary! I laughed and said yes, but I honestly didn't care. I was hired. Off to the academy in November! My adventure of a lifetime was about to start!

2
DEA Academy

"Fortune Favors the Bold" – Latin Proverb.
Also used as the motto for DEA Basic Agent Class #87 of
which I was a member.

I had so much to do before leaving for the academy. I had to let my employer know. I had to do the same with my apartment and the landlord. Plus, I had to move all my furniture and personal belongings into temporary storage. The DEA had sent me a long list of things I would need since I would be living at the academy for 14 weeks. And, most importantly, I had to get in shape. Although I worked out on a regular basis, this was different. This was for my dream job. I saw in the paperwork they sent me that the first Physical Training (PT) test would be given the second day at the academy and if we failed it, we would be put on probation. We would then be given a second chance a few days after and if we failed that one, we would be sent home, no questions asked. This was serious. I proceeded to work out every day. I worked out with weights. I ran. I did wind sprints. I practiced push-ups and sit-ups. Within a matter of weeks, I was in the best shape of my life.... even better than when I reported to summer camp for college football.

Finally, I reported to the academy on November 3, 1991. I remember the sights as I drove through Quantico Marine Base which is where the FBI Academy was located (the DEA did not have its own academy until 1997. So, before that the DEA used the FBI Academy to train their new agents). The U.S. Marines were running everywhere. Alone, in groups, in formations, you name it. And there were gun ranges and rifle ranges everywhere. This was the real deal. I found the FBI Academy, my home for the next 14 weeks, checked in and was assigned a room in a quad suite with two guys to a room and the two rooms connected by a shared bathroom. Needless to say, it was tight..

Our days consisted of breakfast at 6:00 a.m. followed by a PT session. My roommate wasn't an early riser. He hated getting up early so much that he slept in his PT clothes. That way he could sleep until the last minute and then just roll out of bed. Then we had defensive tactics and tactical drills. We would then go back to our rooms and shower after which we had a class or two right up until noon. Sometimes it was legal or law class, sometimes drug identification, or report writing. Then we broke for lunch. Our afternoons were spent at the firing range for anywhere between two to four hours. After that, we broke into groups and either did a mock practical exercise or we trained in Hogan's Alley making entries into houses, learning arrest techniques, conducting vehicle stops and such. Finally, it was dinner time then to our rooms where we would study until lights out. It was like this every day. For 14 weeks! I was exhausted. I was mentally and physically drained. But I guess that was the purpose.

Hogan's Alley was a really cool concept. It's an actual town at the FBI Academy with a bank, a grocery store, a post office and apartments. Normal, right? Maybe. But in this case no one lived there. It was a fake town. It was built so that both FBI agents and DEA agents could learn arrest techniques, search warrant techniques and vehicle stops, in as real an environment as possible. I still couldn't believe this was happening to me. I had to pinch myself. It felt as if I were in a movie or something, like The Silence of the Lambs.

After about two weeks at the academy, we received our first duty assignment. Many people wondered why so early and why the DEA didn't wait to see if we could even make it through and graduate. Well, there was a good reason for this and it was because of the huge expense to send an individual through the academy. I think that I heard one time that it cost about $50,000 per individual after you considered the cost of meals, the accommodations for the class (there were 42 individuals in my class), and the salaries that the academy had to pay to the instructors all for 14 weeks. So, in order not to waste money, your first duty station was assigned in the second week because if you didn't want to live in that city or state and were going to quit and just go home, it was better in the second week than in the second to last week after almost all of that $50,000 had been spent. People did refuse to accept their duty station and quitting did happen. I saw it with an individual in my class. One of the things we had to agree to before starting the academy, and we even had to sign our names agreeing to it, was a Mobility Agreement saying that we would accept an assignment anywhere in the United States. For me, a single guy at the time and living in an apartment, it wasn't that big of a deal. But to someone with a spouse and maybe even kids waiting back home in a house where they had lived for years and in the same town as both of their families, it was a pretty big deal. It was not that the DEA did it on purpose and if there was an opening in our home DEA office, we'd most likely get it. But that couldn't be guaranteed. It was what was referred to as, and this was one of the most popular sayings in the federal government, "the needs of the agency."

The day finally arrived to receive our first official duty station. At that time, they let us make a 'wish list' of where we would like to go. This list was then discussed with one of the class counselors beforehand. A class counselor was a DEA agent who was assigned to live at the academy and mentor the class. After the class graduated, the agent (counselor) returned to the field. When the next class went through, a solicitation went out to the field requesting volunteers to be a class counselor. I knew before meeting with my counselor that the DEA Boston Field Division was closed for new agents. They actually had an overage of agents and were not taking any out of the academy. So, since Boston was where I considered home at the time, I had to formulate a new plan. I had the following on my wish list when I met with the class counselor: The DEA New York Field Division, the DEA New Jersey Field Division and the DEA Philadelphia Field Division. Why these offices? Well, both my parents were originally from New Jersey so I had a ton of relatives living in both New York and New Jersey, including my grandparents. And as far as Philadelphia was concerned, it was only a few hours away from the Boston area which, again, was where I called home at the time. As soon as the counselor saw DEA New York on my list, he freaked out and told me to take it off. He started ranting and raving about the cost of living in New York City, the traffic, the crowds, and the hordes of people living there. He told me I would definitely get DEA New York as that office **always** needs agents. I calmed him down and told him that I knew all that and that I had been to New York a lot in my life. I knew what to expect. And I liked the city! Plus, I wanted to go to a big office where I could learn and experience everything as a young, new agent. I had been hearing that we really learned the job quickly in a big city. We'd see everything within our first year. And so, New York stayed on there.

They made decision day a really dramatic event. They had us all sitting in the classroom and then they would call us out to another room down the hall, one by one. Upon returning to the classroom, each individual stood in front of the class and told the class where he or she was going. And then the class would either applaud or boo or console the individual depending on if the duty station was a good or bad thing. So, I finally went in. They read my choices out loud to me and then without hesitation told me that I've been assigned to the DEA Miami Field Division. Um, sorry. What? Huh? Say what now? It wasn't even on the list. It wasn't even close. But hey, it was late November in Quantico, Virginia, and it was in the 80s in Miami. Plus, it was a big city with plenty of work. A DEA agent could work around the clock there. And, of course, there was Miami Vice! Maybe I could live on a boat with an alligator and drive a Ferrari Daytona Spider! Anyway, back to reality. I soon found out that the wish list was just an attempt to make you feel like you had a say in the decision. The bottom line was that the DEA sent us wherever they needed agents, regardless of where you were from. It was all up to the needs of the agency. See? There's that phrase again. And how do I know about this wish-list flim-flam shim-sham scam? A female in my class put the **exact** same offices as I did on her wish list as she was from the Boston area too. Subsequently, she was assigned to the DEA Las Vegas, NV District Office. Another individual in my class was assigned to the DEA Des Moines, IA Resident Office. And when he came back into the class to announce where he was going, he started by asking where Des Moines was! He didn't even know what state it was in.

But I made it through. I kept my head down and my mouth shut. I soon learned that we should never volunteer for anything in the government. One day during the first week of class one of the instructors asked if anyone had ever worked in a gym. I raised my hand and said that I had, hoping for some kind of bonus points like maybe I wouldn't have to get up at 6:00 a.m. and work out with everyone else and could sleep late. Sorry. Not happening. I was told that I would be responsible for **leading** the class through PT every morning. Great, just great. Another student didn't learn from my over eagerness. The same instructor asked if anyone had ever worked in a post office. This poor guy raised his hand and found himself responsible for collecting the classes' mail every day and handing it out. Woof. And there were 42 people in my class!

My academy class was made up of people from all over the United States and even a few from Puerto Rico. It was interesting being around people from different parts of the country. We all used different words and phrases. We all had different accents. For example, during one night-time practical exercise, I was teamed with an individual from California. We were conducting surveillance on one of the instructors who was role playing as a drug dealer. The individual from California was driving and I was the passenger. Somehow during the surveillance, we ended up way ahead of the mock drug dealer. So, I said to my classmate that we should just pull over on the shoulder of the highway until the vehicle we were supposed to be following had caught up to us. Then we could let him pass and then slip in behind him and re-join the surveillance. So, that's what we did. However, as we pulled off on the shoulder, I looked out the passenger side window and noticed a very steep drop off. I said out loud, "There is a huge gully!" and "Be careful, watch out for the gully!" and "Don't get too close to the edge because of the gully!" I must have said the word gully three or four times. Anyway, we kept going and to my horror, the shoulder gave way and down the embankment we slid. We had to then get on the radio and call ourselves off surveillance. Then the academy had to call us a tow truck. It was quite embarrassing. And it took all night long.

After I had cooled down a bit, I asked my classmate from California why he kept driving along the edge of the shoulder when I kept warning him of the gully. He turned to me and said, "I have no idea what a gully is. I've never even heard of that word." I couldn't help but laugh. I don't know, maybe it's a New England word.

After studying hard, staying healthy, practicing firearms whenever I could (I attended every session, even the make-up sessions and remedial ones, although I wasn't required to since I was a very good shot) and performing well in the practical exercises, I graduated number four in my class on February 14, 1992 with my badge, my credentials, and my gun. I was off to Miami!

3
April, 1992

My first memory was the drive down to Miami. I started in Springfield, Massachusetts, a few days prior. I made stops to visit my grandmother in New Jersey and my sister in Washington, D.C. Then I started down 95 South. I remember after passing through states like Massachusetts, Connecticut and New Jersey, in a matter of hours, how long it took to drive through Virginia, North Carolina and South Carolina. I drove by miles and miles of flat farmland. I remember how the trees changed, the vegetation change, even the air changed. It smelled funny. It smelled damp which I didn't even know was possible. I remember finally reaching South Florida and how exotic it was compared to what I was used to. Even though it was April, the air was already thick and moist. It took my breath away. It was a little "close" as Southerners like to say.

And the trees. Now every tree was a palm tree – a Majesty Palm, a Windmill Palm, a Bottle Palm. It was so flat too. Nothing like New Hampshire where I had grown up. A constant breeze was also present. It never let up. It was a strange land to me, a 25-year-old who had never been this far south in his life. The farthest south I had ever been up to that point was a trip to Daytona Beach for spring break in college one year. I thought that was the edge of the world at that time in my life. But I was now much farther south than that. I remember that my car at the time was a 1987 Nissan Sentra and didn't have air conditioning. Why would it? I saved a bundle opting for no A/C since living in New Hampshire meant one week of humid weather in the summer and then a steady decline in temperatures until the following summer. Then a quick two months of summer and it was over. I drove the last half day from Orlando to Miami with all of the windows down while leaning forward in my seat so that my soaked shirt didn't stick to my back. I tried to angle myself in the driver's seat so that the air coming in from the windows would flow through my short sleeve shirt and hopefully make it to my back. After a couple hours of that, I had to stop at a rest area and walk so that the kink in my back would go away.

And I remember being nervous. Finally, I was a DEA agent! I had just graduated from the academy after 14 long weeks in Quantico, Virginia. And I had graduated number four in my class. I was assigned to Miami, Florida. I was going to be the next Sonny Crockett and dreamt about living on a boat, driving a Ferrari Daytona Spider and then a Ferrari Testarossa. But that was during the idle time in Springfield. It was during that three-month period after graduating from the DEA academy that the Federal Government gave you to "get your affairs in order" as they put it. What the hell did that mean? I never knew. I was 25, and I didn't have any "affairs." But now it was real because I was reporting for duty in a couple of days, in a land that I had never before visited, only having read about it and seeing it on TV. I didn't know a soul, just a stranger in a strange land as they say.

This was 1992. The 80s had just ended and in Miami, the 80s was a blood-filled, brutal period of time when the Medellin Cartel ran **everything.** Bodies turned up on a daily basis. There were shootouts daily. And in places like supermarkets! Kilograms of cocaine seemed to fall out of the sky. The local Federal Reserve had a huge surplus of money. Funeral homes couldn't keep up. I digress. Anyway, I knew them all. I knew all the cocaine cowboys, Pablo Escobar, Carlos Lehder, Griselda Blanco, the Ochoa brothers. And now I was encroaching on their territory. It was pretty heady stuff for a kid who had never fired a weapon before the academy but now strapped a Sig Sauer 9mm semi-automatic pistol to my waist. To be honest, it was pretty scary shit for a rube who had never even been a police officer before. Fuck, I had never even lived alone before! I was shitting bricks. I was in Miami.

4

Special Agent Leighton Gets His First OGV

One nice perk about the job as a special agent (and that applied to whether you were with the DEA, FBI, ATF, etc., it didn't matter) was that we were assigned a take-home vehicle upon reporting to our home office. This car in government-ease was referred to as an Official Government Vehicle, hereafter referred to as an OGV, which was commonly referred to by agents as their "G-Ride" and was a perk that continued for your entire career. It was a huge benefit and one that saved the agent at least $10,000 a year as the government paid for the gas and all maintenance and repairs,not to mention the fact that you weren't using your own personal car to get to and from work. The main reason that the government provided an OGV was that we, as agents, were on call 24/7 and were required to respond at any hour to any enforcement situation. And we needed to have a vehicle available at all times. This way when the call came in, the "My wife is working third shift as a nurse and she has the family car," wouldn't fly. We always had a vehicle ready and available.

Additionally, the work we did was extremely hard on a vehicle. We sat on surveillance, sometimes for hours, sometimes for days with engines running, heat blasting or air conditioning cranked depending on where we lived and the time of year. We occasionally got into car chases. We were also required to run a red light from time to time although this was not encouraged and very dangerous. More than one agent has attempted this and paid dearly. I'm one of them. One time, I was in a long line of cars on the way to execute a federal search warrant in Miami when the light turned red on us as we approached the intersection. Half of the vehicles had made it through while half did not. Unfortunately, I was one of the vehicles that did not. It was imperative that the team all stuck together as we arrived at the target of the search warrant. This was for safety as well as the element of surprise and so that we all would arrive at the residence at the same time. We could then approach the front door as a unit and make entry together. Anyway, I ran the light. I activated my lights and siren and proceeded with caution. Unfortunately, someone coming the opposite way somehow did not see the emergency lights on my vehicle nor did they hear the siren. So, I was t-boned. I was a bit shaken up but not seriously hurt. It could have been much worse. Needless to say, I did not make the search warrant that day.

Any time we moved with the government we got what was referred to as administrative days or "admin" days. These were so that you we could get our "affairs in order" (there was that phrase again) and got things like cable hooked up, furniture moved into our houses or apartments, children enrolled in school (if agents had children). Miscellaneous tasks like that. One of these was to repot to our new office and pick-up our OGV. Then we would leave and report back in our OGV for our official first day of duty after we had burned our admin. days. I did this, as well, as soon as I arrived in Miami. I remember that I was given a Chevrolet Corsica. I don't think they make those anymore but it was a nice vehicle. It was certainly better than my 1987 Nissan Sentra without A/C! I returned to my apartment and began my admin. days and the task of moving in and getting settled.

All was going well. My first official day had arrived. I was excited and petrified all at the same time. I left my apartment early so that I would have plenty of time to drive to work. I had the directions to the office written down after studying an old paper map (no internet, cell phones, GPSs or any type or Google maps in 1992) the night before. I started my drive from Plantation, which was where my apartment was, to Miami. Plantation was just west of Ft. Lauderdale so it would take me approximately 45 minutes to make the drive to the office. It was a pleasant morning in late April. I decided to roll down my window instead of use the air conditioning since it was so nice outside. I had never been able to do that in April having lived in the Northeast the majority of my life so I wanted to enjoy it.

As I got closer to the office, I remember noticing that some of the highway billboards were in Spanish only, while driving on the Palmetto Expressway. I remember asking myself, "What have I done?" I passed billboards for products like Miller Lite but the caption was in Spanish only. About this time, while shaking my head and wondering if I was still in the United States, traffic started getting heavier as I got closer to the DEA Miami, FL Field Division. The directions that I had with me were resting on my knee so that I could just look down and follow them. All of a sudden, as I slowed down to exit, a tractor trailer blew by me. The directions that were on my lap were suddenly relocated to the floor of my car, and not on my side but on the passenger's side! Instead of remembering that I had built in plenty of time and should have pulled over, I decided to reach over as far as I could to grab them. I got them but as I straightened back up, I proceeded to smash into the car in front of me who had stopped abruptly in traffic. I was horrified. What now? There was a part of me that actually considered calling it a day. Shortest stint as a Special Agent in DEA history! I finally collected myself, exchanged information with the other driver and continued on my journey.... this time almost in tears.

As I entered the DEA lobby, the receptionist asked where I was going. I told her that I had no idea. I told her who I was and that I was reporting for the first day. She looked up my name and made a phone call. Before I knew it, an agent was taking me to my new group. Imagine the horror meeting my fellow agents and then explaining that I had just been in an accident. I remember like it was yesterday. I called it a fender bender. The Group Supervisor at the time came out with me to take a look. I'll never forget his comment,

"That's one hell of a fender bender."

So instead of settling into my new desk, meeting all the agents or participating in surveillances or arrests or search warrants, I was tasked with getting estimates from garages and completing an accident package. One of the senior agents who could see I was down and depressed told me that it was bound to happen at some point and that Miami had the worst drivers anywhere in the U.S. He then added that at least I would know how to complete the paperwork the next time that I had an accident. The funniest part of this story, at least looking back at it now and not at the time, was that when the accident package made its way to senior management for approval, the Assistant Special Agent in Charge asked, "Who is this person? I've never heard of him. Is he even in our office?" And one final comment. I was assigned another OGV later that day. Like I stated previously, every agent gets a car regardless. Even if the agent was a jackass and crashed his OGV on his first day of work! So, I was now assigned a 1988 Chevy Caprice, a boat of a car...that had no AC!! Karma!!

5
May 1992

After completing my first OGV accident package, and certainly not my last, it was time to get focused on my new group and career and get to work. My first assignment in Miami was with the Transportation Group. This group specialized in maritime smuggling – mainly cocaine, as that was the drug of choice in Miami at that time. The Transportation Group used human assets (government lingo for informants) who were well positioned in South America in port cities like Cartagena and Barranquilla. These informants worked the docks, hung out in bars in the ports listening and picking up whatever bits of conversations and overhears that they could. They would then either pass on the information to the local DEA office who, in turn, would forward the information to us, or they would communicate directly with our group in Miami, usually through one of our already established informants in Miami. We would then forward whatever information we received to our local maritime counterparts, agencies like U.S. Customs, U.S. Coast Guard and our own intelligence center in El Paso, affectionately called E.P.I.C. – the El Paso Intelligence Center. These counterparts would then start tracking these vessels as they moved slowly through the Atlantic Ocean up toward the Port of Miami which was usually the final destination.

After tracking the vessel for days and sometimes weeks, we would then request through U.S. Customs that the U.S. Coast Guard perform a boarding of the vessel. This was something that the U.S. Coast Guard could do anytime they liked without any evidence or probable cause. They were allowed to do this due to their mission of protecting our waters, U.S. ports, the U.S. coastline, and U.S. natural borders. The first case I participated in, which was given to me to work on since I was the "newbie," resulted in a seizure of multi-hundred kilograms of cocaine from the Motor Vessel *Sebastian*. Pretty heavy stuff for my first case.

Here I am (third from the right) with agents from the Miami Office alongside the Motor Vessel (M/V) Sebastian

6
Summer 1992

"For those who fight for it, life has a flavor the protected
will never know"
– Theodore Roosevelt.

This quote was also inscribed on the back of a protective vest worn by a machine-gunner in the demilitarized zone between North and South Vietnam in 1968. Also, this inscription was engraved on a plaque outside the Group 9 office in the DEA Miami Field Division as a token of appreciation from the **1st Special Forces Operational Detachment-Delta** commonly referred to as **Delta Force**, the U.S. Marine detachment that surrounded the Nunciature until General Manuel Noriega surrendered after 10 days of sanctuary.

Although I was enjoying myself in the Transportation Group, I have to admit that I was a lit-tle bored. Instead of chasing drug dealers, making arrests and seizures on the mean streets of Miami, I found myself tracking huge maritime freighters. I spent a good deal of the day on the phone with our maritime assets getting new coordinates, plotting the travel on a map, and trying to decide the best time to intercept and board the vessel. But I was young, in shape, and I carried a badge and a gun. I wanted more. Then came the break I needed. The upper management of the Miami office decided that some of the groups needed to be re-aligned. Some had too many senior agents. Others had too many young agents. As a result, a number of personnel were moved around including me! I was transferred to a group that had been in existence since 1989 but was being transformed into a regular enforcement group.

This group had previously been the Noriega Prosecution Group, as in General Manuel Noriega. It was Group 9. My home for the next seven years.

On December 20, 1989, as part of Operation Just Cause, the U.S. invaded the country of Panama to dethrone and topple the government of General Manuel Noriega. After years of excellent cooperation between Panama and the U.S., the DEA, CIA and State Department grew weary of all of the talk about the corrupt behavior of General Noriega. The four big "Is of any law enforcement entity – Intelligence, Information, Investigation and Informants had all been saying for years that General Noriega was a high-level drug trafficker and had amassed a fortune from drug trafficking. Additionally, he had very close ties with the Medellin Cartel in Colombia and had rou-tinely allowed the cartel to utilize the numerous banks in Panama to facilitate their narcotics money laundering activities. Eventually, General Noriega was indicted by a federal grand jury in both Tampa, Florida and Miami, Florida for racketeering, drug trafficking and money laundering. Subsequently, following the invasion, General Noriega was flown to Miami where he was tried for the Miami indictment.

General Noriega was eventually found guilty and a sentencing date had been set. However, preparing for any trial was an arduous task, not to mention a trial in which a disposed general from a foreign country was on trial. This was where the Noriega Prosecution Team came in. Since General Noriega had been indicted by a federal grand jury for offenses related to drug trafficking, it only made sense to turn to the DEA Miami Office to assist the U.S Attorney's Office in preparing for trail. So that's what they did. For almost two years, DEA agents assigned to Group 9 traveled the world interviewing witnesses and preparing them for trial. It could not have been done without them. They worked seven days a week. They spent days, nights, and weekends away from their families. And this is where I came in. The very week I was assigned to this group was the week of the General Noriega sentencing. It was in the main courtroom of the Miami Federal Courthouse. It was packed, and I was there. I remember noticing how short Noriega was but at the same time how he terrified me. The nickname "Pineapple Face" did fit the bill. I remember that I found it odd that although deposed and lacking any kind of military power or authority, he was still allowed to wear his military uniform throughout the trail and the sentencing. So, there he was in his uniform and military regalia looking like a beaten man, head hung low.

When it came time to make a statement before receiving his sentence, Noriega stood and proceeded to talk straight for two hours! He basically attacked the United States, President George H.W. Bush and the U.S. Marines. He spoke of being a prisoner of war, having immunity, and how his arrest violated international law. The entire diatribe was in Spanish but even with my limited knowledge of Spanish, I could make out enough words to know that he was blaming *everything* on the United States. The impassioned speech did not work. When he finished, the judge proceeded to sentence General Noriega to 40 years' incarceration. What a thrill it was just to be in that room. Again, I felt just like a kid. And here, Noriega was in the same room as me. More importantly and more about this later, but that day I met a young, aggressive Assistant United States Attorney (AUSA) who was considered a legal savant and would eventually be a huge force in the development of my career as an agent.

7
The Shooting

Often in a large office like Miami, we were asked to assist other groups with enforcement operations. Usually, it was to provide perimeter security if the operation was a search warrant at a residence. Or maybe it was assisting with booking and processing prisoners if the group in which we were assisting did a round up and arrested a bunch of people. So, it was usually in a back-up role assignment while the agents in the main group took on the primary function of the operation. And as the new guy in the group, I was often asked to assist other groups which I didn't mind doing at all because it was an opportunity to experience more enforcement which I couldn't get enough of in those days. I was asked to assist in what we referred to as a buy-bust. A buy-bust operation was when an informant or undercover agent bought a certain quantity of drugs from a drug dealer and as soon as the transaction was completed, the arrest team would move in and arrest or "bust" the drug dealer. It was a very common operation and probably the most popular within the DEA. However, instead of being placed on the perimeter team as mentioned earlier, or back in the office waiting to process prisoners, I was actually put on the arrest team since I was new, and they wanted me to get some experience actually arresting someone and putting handcuffs on a real person instead of a tackling dummy or, even worse, on each other as we did at the academy in Quantico. I couldn't wait. It would be my first tactical situation and arrest since being assigned to the Miami office!

Just a little background on the actual scenario. It was going to be a five-kilogram cocaine buy-bust operation utilizing an informant. It was a very common operation, but this one had a twist. Normally these types of operations were always done in a public place, like a parking lot at Wal-Mart or Home Depot. That was for our safety. We made it a rule to never go inside a residence to buy drugs or make an arrest. There were too many unknowns. There was always the possibility of a rip off, or an ambush, or people hiding in closets, or in a spare room. We made it a habit of having 100% control of the environment in which we were working. We had a saying in the DEA that every agent knew and it was the first thing that was taught at the academy, and it was that everyone went home at night. There was no drug dealer, or amount of drugs, or amount of cash, or any seizure that was worth someone getting hurt. We took great pride in walking away from ANY operation if we felt it was unsafe or could get someone hurt, or worse, killed.

However, in this particular operation the informant actually asked the case agents if the transaction could be done inside the informant's residence. At first, this request was met with a resounding no. Again, we never did an operation inside a house. It was just something we didn't do. However, this was different. This was the informant's house. The informant worked for us. And we could always go in the house before the transaction and check every spare room, every closet and every nook and cranny. We had to be safe and sure. Because even though the informant worked for us, it wouldn't be the first time that an informant went south on us. Every agent has had a "rogue" informant or a "broken arrow" informant. But if we declared the house to be safe, it could actually help us make the arrest. We could control the environment. We could have the arrest team right around the corner in the house. In this case the transaction was supposed to take place in the kitchen, and we could be right around the corner in the dining room. When the kilograms of cocaine were handed to the informant, he was to tell the drug dealer that the money was inside his bedroom and that he would be right back after getting it. That way the informant would be out of the way when the arrest was made. And how would we know when the transaction was consummated? In every situation like this, we used what was referred to as an arrest signal. In this case, we told the informant that when the five kilograms of cocaine were handed to the informant and he proceeded to leave the room to retrieve the money, the informant was to say "Perfecto" just as the informant was leaving. Then we would know that the transaction was complete and we could move in to make the arrest. Sounds simple, right? Wrong.

Everything up to this point was going fine. We had agents on perimeter around the house in their vehicles waiting for the drug dealer, or what we referred to as the target, to arrive. After they watched him walk in the informant's residence, they were to proceed to outside of the residence to make sure the target didn't run if the arrest went sideways for any reason. The arrest team, including myself, was geared up and ready to go inside the dining room. The informant was hanging out inside the kitchen waiting for the target to arrive. All was good.

Eventually the target arrived and proceeded to the residence. And he was carrying a bag which was always a good sign since five kilograms of cocaine could not be stuffed in a pocket or shoved down one's pants. The informant answered the door and let the target in. The agents on perimeter exited their vehicles and proceeded cautiously to the outside of the residence covering each window and door while making sure the target didn't see them if he looked outside. The target and the informant first engaged in some idle chit chat. Then the conversation switched to the task at hand. It was the normal drug conversation about the purity, the possibility of getting more in the future, the price and if the price could be lowered if the informant purchased more cocaine the next time. It sounded like a typical business conversation except this one centered on a slightly different commodity – five kilograms of cocaine. After a few minutes we heard what we had been waiting for, the word "Perfecto." We moved in.

When an arrest was made, it was a fairly simple procedure. Five or six agents all in a line basically approached the target shouting commands like "Police! Don't move," "Hands up" and the obvious "You're under arrest." Additionally, we always had an agent with us on the arrest team who was a native Spanish speaker saying the same phrases but in Spanish to make sure there wasn't a language barrier. Phrases like "Policia," "No te muevas," and "Manos arriba" were shouted at the same time. And, obviously, guns were drawn and vests were on. So, just as we were about to grab the target to place handcuffs on him, which looked like it was going to be pretty routine since the target was just standing there motionless with his hands up, the target quickly reached into the waistband of his pants and... pulled a gun out, placed it under his chin and blew his head off!!

We were in shock. We stood there with guns drawn staring with our mouths wide open as we were all in shock with what we had just witnessed. There was blood everywhere and brain matter on the kitchen wall behind the target. To make matters worse and the situation even more confusing, the agents on perimeter, thinking that the target must be firing at the arrest team, stormed the house as they were supposed to in this situation, kicking in the door and breaking windows, basically whatever they had to do to get into the house as quickly as possible to help their fellow agents. It was a crazy scene. And seeing us with guns drawn and the target dead on the kitchen floor with a gun next to him on the floor, the agents on the perimeter team started reassuring us and saying stuff like, "Don't worry," or "It was a good shoot," or "He had a gun. You had to do it," since anyone in law enforcement who carries a weapon was justified in shooting a target if the target took a shot at us or even just points a gun our way. The ironic thing is that I remember saying to one of the agents who was trying to calm us down that I never got a shot off since he shot himself. Then it got comical. I panicked, and since I had never been in a situation like this in my entire life or had even seen a dead person in real life, I yelled out, "Someone call 911!"

With a chuckle, one of the senior agents put his hand on my

shoulder trying to calm me down and said, "No, let's just call homicide. There's no need for an ambulance." Obviously, he had seen a dead body or two in his time. Agents could also be a pretty tough crowd or audience. The stress of the job sometimes got the best of us and we needed to relieve it with humor. Otherwise, we'd lose our minds. Just then one of the other senior agents decided to play with the 'new guy' and turned to me and told me to go to my car and get my fingerprint kit since we needed fingerprints from the target so we could claim the arrest stat. I felt really queasy at this point seeing all the blood and guts and brain matter and then noticing that rigor mortis was already setting in. I remember thinking that this was not included in the training at the academy! At that point, the laughter couldn't be contained anymore as everyone in the room but me broke into hysterics at my expense.

In the aftermath, as we tried to figure why this person had done what he did and kill himself, it never ever really added up. To be honest, five kilograms in Miami in the 1990s was not a lot of cocaine. Sure, it met federal guidelines and the target would have done some jail time, but not much. We determined that he was 32 years old and did not have any previous arrests. And after cooperating and pleading guilty, he probably would have been sentenced to about five years in jail. In the federal system you normally do about 80% of your sentence, so he would have done about four years in jail after all was said and done. That's just a blip on the radar screen when you're 32 years old. However, a couple weeks after that, one of the agents told us that he had found out something recently that put a different spin on the matter. This agent had found out that the dead man's mother was a radio dispatcher for the Miami Metro–Dade Police Department. Could that be the reason? Maybe. Shame and embarrassment are two pretty devastating emotions.

8
Duty Agent

Every group and office in DEA, whether a big office like Miami or a small one like Providence, Rhode Island, in which I was assigned from 2002 to 2009, had what was referred to as a Duty Agent for the day, or week, or even month. This person handled random tasks, took the anonymous callers with drug tip information, assisted other groups with surveillance if they were short on personnel, handled requests from other DEA offices, and documented investigative leads from other local police departments. One day, early in my career, I was the designated Duty Agent for my group. Around noon that day, I received a call on the duty line which had been forwarded to my desk phone. It was an individual who stated that he was at the International Mall, which was about 10 minutes from my office. The individual stated that his wife had to make a merchandise return at Macy's and had run into the store quickly while he waited in the car. The individual then stated that he just observed two vehicles in the next row in the parking lot parked side by side with both trunks of the vehicles wide open. The man said that he was watching two individuals trying to get a very large suitcase out of the trunk of the one car and into the trunk of the other car. Then the man added that the suitcase was so heavy that they were having a lot of problems just getting it out of the trunk of the one car.

I found it intriguing and wondered what could be in the suitcase that made it so heavy? I proceeded to ask the man to wait there and told him that a few agents would be responding. I then grabbed a couple of other agents who were hanging around the office at the time and drove over to the mall which, again, was only about 10 minutes away from my office. When we arrived, we located the two cars with the trunks open and the two individuals in question, and believe it or not, they were **still** trying to get that damn suitcase out of the one vehicle. We casually approached them and asked them if they needed help. We were trying to get a measure of their level of nervousness. They quickly refused and went back to their task at hand. We then identified ourselves with our credentials and started asking questions about what they were doing. The two men were visibly shaken and nervous upon learning that the three of us were DEA agents.

We then informed them that we believed that the suitcase contained something illegal and asked for a consent search which is when the owner gives you permission to search the item at hand, for example a residence, or a car, or a suitcase, without having a warrant. They hesitated and looked at one another for answers. Then one said that they would rather us get a warrant. We told the two men that we would but that it would probably be a few hours by the time we went back to the office, wrote the warrant, had it reviewed by the prosecutor, and then tracked down a judge in order to get it signed. We also told the two men that we would have to stay there with the suitcase while all this was happening and that they would not be able to leave the scene. Upon hearing all this they opted for the consent search route. With the consent given, the three of us managed to get the suitcase out of the trunk of the vehicle and on the ground. We proceeded to open it and were flabbergasted upon seeing the contents. Mixed in with the normal assortment of clothes and toiletries that we would usually find in a suitcase were 50 kilograms of cocaine. That's 110 pounds! Only in Miami do you get a duty call that results in two arrests and the seizure of 50 kilograms of cocaine all during our lunch hour.

I had another great duty agent experience and one that came with a nice little reward at the end. One day, I was sitting at my desk when my supervisor walked out and asked who the duty agent was for the day. It was me, so I raised my hand and stated as such. He said that it was just as well since I was the new guy anyway. He informed me that Her Majesty's Customs and Excise (HMCE) in the United Kingdom had an arrest warrant for an individual living in Miami, and they needed some assistance with the lay of the land. He stated that a couple HMCE officers would be arriving the next morning. I was to pick them up at the airport and then take them to the U.S. Attorney's Office where they would use the probable cause in their U.K. arrest warrant and swear out a U.S. Federal Arrest Warrant. We would then come back to the DEA office and meet with analysts in the intelligence group to start determining possible residences in which the target might be residing.

The second day I would pick them up in the morning at their hotel, and we would begin conducting surveillance on the residence that the Intelligence Analysts had found for us. We would wait until we observed him either entering or leaving and then we would affect the arrest. We had a good location, which was a high-rise condo along Biscayne Boulevard, so that's where we would start that morning. Hopefully, this would only take a day or two.

So, on that second day, I picked up the HMCE officers at their hotel and headed out to the condo. We found a decent spot in the parking lot once we arrived – one that gave us a good view of the front door – so, we parked there and waited. A photo of the suspect laid on our laps and with binoculars, we prepared for a long day.

Around lunch time, I came up with a plan. We needed to make sure that this condo was the right location. There was nothing worse to a surveillance agent than to invest a ton of time into a venture if we were at the wrong damn location. Been there, done that. With that being said, I decided to go into the condo and meet with a manager or sales associate and show them the photo.

Yes, this was risky. We never knew who was involved in the drug game. There was always a chance that the person we speak to tells the individual in question that the police were there that day asking about him. However, I found that if we worded it right and made sure that the individuals that the agents were speaking to knew that if they said anything or revealed that agents were there, they could be charged with obstruction of justice. Plus, every once in a while, we just had to take a chance. We were in an unusual occupation. Nothing was like it in the world. We didn't work nine to five. We didn't make widgets. We worked the street. And we had to take chances once in a while – calculated risks.

Well, it worked. The person I spoke to that day recognized the photo and said that the individual did reside there. Whew. We were at the right spot. Now, we just had to wait. And we did. But, as the day went on, my colleagues were tiring. I understood as the six-hour time difference between London and Miami was taking its toll. Plus, the plane ride had been brutal. It was non-stop from London to Miami on Virgin Atlantic. So, I took them back to their hotel so they could get some rest with the plan being that I would pick them up the next morning at their hotel and start all over again. Then I headed back out to the condo.

Conducting surveillance on our own is never a good thing. Many years later, as a supervisor, I strictly enforced this with my agents and Task Force Officers, hereafter referred to as TFOs. By the way, a TFO was actually a detective of another department assigned to DEA for a three to five-year assignment. Anyway, too many bad things could happen. But I was young, foolish, and bullet proof. Well, believe it or not, as soon as I arrived back at the condo and found a parking spot, I saw the individual walk out of the lobby and get in a car to leave the area. How lucky! But as I always said, it's better to be lucky than good in this job. If I had been a few minutes later I would have missed him. I wanted to follow him so that I could grab the vehicle registration and confirm that this was the right person, but I was pretty sure it was. Besides, I was alone and didn't want to burn the surveillance. Additionally, all we had to do the next day was grab him once we saw him leave the lobby. That is, if he'd even leave the next day. We never knew. Some people had whacky schedules. We would find out.

We set up on surveillance the next morning and, after a few

hours, we actually saw the person walk out of the lobby and approach his vehicle. We quickly started our car up and pulled in front of him so that he couldn't leave as he was boxed in with a car on either side of him and in back of him (he had backed into the space). He didn't know what hit him. Within seconds, we were at the driver's side door with guns out and badges asking him to exit the vehicle. He did so and was calm and polite about it. We asked him a couple of questions which he answered. Again, no problem. He confirmed that he was who we had the arrest warrant for so we placed him in custody. No problems or issues at all. It couldn't have gone any smoother.

That was really it. Three days of work. Not bad for a duty agent assignment. The individual that we arrested that day was eventually extradited back to the U.K. to face his charges. I dropped off the HMCE officers at Miami International the next day, and we said our goodbyes. I thought that would be the last that I would ever hear of this story and of the HMCE officers. I was wrong!

About a year later (extraditions take a lot of time) the same supervisor as before came out of his office and asked who was the individual that helped the U.K. make an arrest about a year ago. I somehow had a really good feeling about this, almost a sixth sense, and stated that it was me. To my absolute delight, he stated to pack my bags since they needed the arresting officer to travel to the U.K. for trial. London, here I come!

I remember getting so much grief from the senior agents in the group. It was all about how lucky I was, and why I got to go and not them, and how I should give up the trip, etc. All good-natured ribbing, mind you, nothing malicious. They realized that I took the case, handled it well, and took care of the HMCE guys, therefore, I deserved to go. I gave it right back to them, though, reminding them that I didn't hear anyone volunteering to help the HMCE guys since a trip to London wasn't on the table then. It was all good.

I packed a suitcase and made flight and hotel arrangements. I would be going for a week since they were not sure at what time during the trial I would be testifying. Also, I was told that the U.K. was picking up all expenses for this trip, as they should since it was their investigation, and that I needed to book my flight on a U.K. based airline, not a U.S. based airline. Due to an arrangement between the UK and HMCE, I found myself on a Virgin Atlantic flight a few days later and staying at the London Bridge Hotel. What an opportunity!

To be honest, it was kind of a letdown. Trials in the U.K. are just like trials in the U.S. They are long and unpredictable. I mean, I did the best that I could as far as sightseeing and the HMCE guys were great, taking me out for dinner and drinks every night. But every day while I was there, I would put my suit on in the morning and head to the courthouse to testify. And day after day, I didn't get on the witness stand. I just had to wait my turn. But I couldn't leave in case something schedule-wise happened, and they needed me right away. Trials were so unpredictable. Sure, every prosecutor had a witness list and tried to follow it, but we'd never know the issues that could come up during witness testimony, or how long the defense counsels planned to take on cross examination, or what they would pull out of their sleeves. It's completely fluid. Sometimes the prosecutor, depending on how the trial was going, would often flip flop witnesses for whatever reason.

I spent my first three days hanging out in the courthouse. On day four, I finally got on the stand which resulted in a funny but also embarrassing moment for me. When I entered the court room, I noticed that the prosecutor, defense counsel, and judge all had wigs on! They looked like George Washington or Thomas Jefferson from my old history books. This really threw me off. And they weren't even trying to hide the fact that they had hair underneath. They just had these wigs lying on top of their heads. That kind of struck me as odd. Soon after, I learned that this was just a historical nod or recognition of U.K. history as this was simply the fashion back then.

I proceeded up to the witness stand to get sworn in. Nothing new. So far so good. I had done this many times in my career by then. But then it happened. I entered the witness stand or box and immediately noticed that there wasn't a chair or seat. *Hmm,* I thought. *Is there a jump seat or murphy seat that folds down from the side?* So, I started rubbing my hands along the inside walls of the witness box thinking, *where is this damn seat?* Just then the judge noticed me doing this and asked what I was doing. I almost died from embarrassment. Sheepishly, I told the judge I was trying to find the seat. He just looked at me from under his white wig and over his bifocals and informed me that in the U.K., witnesses stand when they testify. I was mortified. So, I stood the entire time. **Don't you think someone could have given me a heads up on this?**

That wasn't the most embarrassing part of my trip, believe it or not. On my final full day there, one of the HMCE officers felt bad for me since I had been holed up in a dingy courthouse for most of the week. He decided to drive me around and quickly show me the sights. It wasn't as good as exploring all of these amazing sites in person, but I knew that he was doing the best that he could, so I appreciated it. While he drove me around, I saw Buckingham Palace, Harrod's, London Bridge, Trafalgar Square, Big Ben, 10 Downing Street, and the House of Parliament to name a few. Just when we were about out of time, he turned to me in the car and asked if I wanted to see Scotland Yard. I literally said out loud to him, "I do, but you just said we don't have much time, so I don't think we have enough time to drive to Scotland." Honest to goodness. You should have seen the look on his face. It was priceless. He didn't know what to say to this simpleton sitting next to him in the car. I was beside myself when he told me that Scotland Yard wasn't in the country of Scotland but in London and referred to the name of the headquarters building of the Metropolitan Police. At that point in my career, I had not become the international traveler that I am now, obviously, and, man, did it show!

9
Elephants, Not Antelopes

*"Here in Miami, this is the land of elephants, and we hunt elephants,
we don't hunt antelopes"*
– Former Special Agent in Charge of the DEA Miami Field Division.

Around 1993, a couple of senior agents got together and decided that it was time to get me started on my own investigation. They gave me one of their informants to use. In turn, the informant came up with a target. This target was a small–time drug dealer, selling grams and ounces of cocaine which was very small stuff for Miami at that time, or any time actually. But it didn't matter. I was going to have a chance to run an informant, to run an operation, to collect evidence, to formulate an operational plan, to plan out the arrest, and to be the lead agent at the prosecution table if the target decided to go to trial after the arrest. It was going to be my show from beginning to end. And these cases, albeit small and probably inconsequential to an area like Miami, are vital and extremely important to the education, upbringing and development of a new agent.

With all that being said, the investigation was completed after about a month. The informant first met with the target to tell the target that an individual had approached him asking where he could get some cocaine. Subsequently, the informant introduced this individual, actually a DEA undercover agent, to the target. They negotiated back and forth about amounts, prices, and purities for about a week or so and finally decided on an amount and price. A few buy-walk operations were then completed. These were operations where we bought a certain amount and number of drugs from an individual but let the target walk away. He or she wasn't arrested at that time. We would normally do two or three of these operations during the course of the investigation. The reason this was done was to show a pattern, a definite overt act, a continued series of crimes – which was selling drugs to someone over and over – and not just a one-time deal.

Eventually, with a few buy-walk operations under our belt, we planned a buy-bust operation. As I mentioned earlier, a buy-bust operation is where we'd buy a certain amount of drugs from an individual but this time the individual was arrested. The buy-bust operation went down without a hitch. Everything went as planned. We made the arrest. We prosecuted the individual and he immediately started cooperating. There wasn't a trial so it was a pretty quick investigation. Again, just a small-time drug dealer was arrested but the experience to a young agent like me was immeasurable.

One day, I received a call from the Special Agent in Charge (SAC) of the entire office. He asked me to come see him in his office. I remember thinking that I was screwed. What had I done? With a queasy stomach, I proceeded to his office. Once there, he asked me to sit down and tell him about this case that I had just completed. I remember wondering how he knew about this investigation since the Miami office had about 150 agents assigned to it at that time. Anyway, I proceeded to tell him about the investigation. He sat there nodding and listening attentively. When I was finished, he simply responded with this one line. I always remembered it throughout my career and it still makes me laugh. He said that I had done a great job and that he was proud of me, but to always remember that this was Miami and "Here in Miami, this is the land of elephants, and we hunt elephants, we don't hunt antelopes."

At first, I had no idea what he was talking about. Then I figured it out. This is the DEA Miami Office. Best of the best in DEA. We hunt the big drug dealers here, the king pins. We have way too many big targets (elephants) to be concerned with the small-time drug dealers (antelopes). It was a good point and one that I always remembered during my time in Miami. Lesson learned. Time to step up my game!

10
La Guajira

"Plans are nothing; Planning is everything"
– Dwight D. Eisenhower

One of the first major cases that I had as a young agent was when I was assigned to work with an agent in my group whose name was Greg. He was my senior partner at the time and since he had been a sergeant with a local Florida Police Department for many years pre-DEA, he was an excellent role model. It turned out that Greg had graduated from the academy with another agent who was assigned to the New Jersey office, an agent by the name of Scott.

One day Scott called Greg and told him that he had an informant who had been contacted by a high-level marijuana trafficking organization in Colombia. Scott explained that the reason the informant had been contacted was that the informant was a pilot and the Colombian organization needed someone to fly a load of marijuana from the La Guajira area of Colombia to Miami. Scott told Greg that he was more than welcome to use this informant if he wanted in order to try to complete this investigation. Greg jumped at the chance. He had only been with the DEA about a year more than I had, so he was a super aggressive agent like myself and, additionally, he had been one of the original agents in the Noriega Prosecution Group. So, after all of that trial prep, he was chomping at the bit to do some real enforcement work.

The first task was meeting the informant. That was relatively easy. We proceeded to contact the informant via a telephone call, and the informant was very amenable to traveling down to Miami to meet with Greg and me. After we had paid for the flight and hotel, the informant was in Miami a few days later meeting with us. We started with what we would do with any informant – conduct a full detailed debriefing. We usually started the same by asking the informant to take us through the entire scenario from when the informant first spoke to the members of the Colombian organization to every transaction that the informant conducted with any members of the organization after that. This was crucial because in our line of work, one small, missed detail or an omission could mean the difference between life and death. After sitting down with us for hours and hours, we had pretty much everything we needed as far as knowing exactly who we were dealing with.

The next step was obtaining a plane. This was a little more difficult since planes were expensive. We had the informant reach out to the members of the organization and request that they pay for the plane. The informant was a free-lance pilot, so it wasn't expected that the informant would own his own plane. A few days after this phone call, the informant was contacted and instructed to meet with a representative from the Colombian organization in Miami. Believe it or not, this individual proceeded to give our informant a brown paper bag full of cash that the informant was to use to buy the plane. I had never seen so much money in my life! And all cash! Buying a plane sounded like a daunting task but I quickly learned that a pilot would know what to do and what to look for. It'd be no different than me buying a car. And in an area like Miami, there were a number of brokers whose primary job was to sell used aircraft. With the informant by our side and a bag of cash, we started shopping for a plane. After visiting Miami International Airport and Opa Locka Airport, we found one that the informant said would work. Now we had a plane.

Just a side note about the bag of cash. The plane was purchased with our money, DEA money. Whenever an informant received funding from a drug trafficking organization that was to be used to buy something like a car, or a plane, or a boat, or even a phone that would be used to facilitate a crime, it was immediately seized and put into evidence because it was an overt act in the overall criminal conspiracy. That was the first nail in the coffin. And then we turned around and used our own funding to purchase the item at hand – this time, a plane. It sounded like a huge expenditure, but if we already had the seized cash on hand and we knew that it would be administratively seized and forfeited once the investigation was over and all judicial proceedings had been settled, it was much easier of a sell to the bosses and upper management. It was basically a wash.

Next came negotiating with the Colombians. This actually took a while since it involved heavy logistics. Flying an airplane from Miami to Colombia, landing on a dirt makeshift runway, loading bales of marijuana on the plane and then flying back to Miami was no easy task. There was much to discuss and negotiate. Luckily, our informant spoke Spanish so that was a huge advantage. Also, having a pilot as our informant really assisted in the negotiations since not everyone can fly a plane, and pilots willing to work for drug trafficking organizations are few and far between. That basically gave us the upper hand and after a couple weeks of phone calls and negotiations, it was set.

Greg and I had our work cut out for us, as well. We needed to coordinate with headquarters in Washington, D.C., the Bogota, Colombia office, the U.S. Coast Guard and the U.S. Customs Service. This was an undercover operation involving an undercover aircraft piloted by a documented DEA informant in an official DEA investigation. The last thing we needed was for the plane to pop up on U.S. Coast Guard or U.S. Customs radar systems and they hadn't been apprised of the operation. Everyone needed to be on board. As Greg said to me one time with a sly smile just before the operation started, "What could go wrong?"

It was decided that the informant would leave at night and

make the trip from Miami to the La Guajira section of Colombia. The informant would land, and the plane would then be loaded with 15,000 pounds of marijuana by members of the Colombian organization. We would be in the DEA radio room in Miami communicating with the informant on a secure channel so that we would know exactly what was happening. The informant would then fly back to Miami and land at Opa Locka airport. Hence, the plan was set.

However, before I continue, Dwight D. Eisenhower once said, "Plans are nothing; Planning is everything." After nearly 30 years with DEA, I now understand that. But I wish I did when I was 25 years old. We had a plan. We had agreed on what we wanted to happen. That's a plan. But planning incorporates the 'what ifs' and the 'buts' and the myriad of other unknowns.

The first disaster was that the radio communication failed. We had no comms with the informant. I wasn't sure if the range was simply too far, or if had to do with our radio in the radio room, or the radio in the plane, but we couldn't communicate that entire night with the informant. That was a nightmare.

The second potential disaster was that no one thought beforehand of determining how much the plane would weigh after the marijuana had been loaded and if the plane would be able to get off the ground. Obviously, Greg and I weren't physics majors. To make matters worse, apparently the airstrip was along a cliff. The informant told us after the fact that when the plane was barreling down the runway for takeoff, the informant couldn't get the wheels of the plane off the ground. With the runway ending in a matter of seconds and with nothing but cliffs, rocks and ocean below, the informant had absolutely no idea if the plane was going to remain airborne when the runway ran out, or if the plane would just hurl down in a horrific crash. When the runway finally ran out, to the shock of the informant, the plane remained airborne and continued to fly. It was an absolute miracle.

After a long night of flying, and us being totally in the dark wondering if the informant had even made it, or if the plane had been loaded with the marijuana along with a host of other questions and concerns, the plane landed at Opa Locka airport. It was October 1, 1992. We had the entire rest of the group out there to off-load the marijuana for transport to our lab. It was a long night, but I remember how astounded I was to see what 15,000 pounds of marijuana looked like.

I'd like to say that the story ended on a happy note, but it didn't. Some investigations simply don't work out or don't get to the level that you had hoped for when the investigation was initiated. There are just so many factors that come into play. In this case, we were supposed to make a delivery of the 15,000 pounds of marijuana to the representatives of the Colombian organization that lived and operated in Miami.

15,000 pounds of Marijuana transported from the La Guajira area of Colombia

After weeks of negotiations, an agreement on the transfer of the marijuana could not be decided. Our new informant, an undercover agent who we were able to introduce to the organization, and the organization members in Miami couldn't agree upon a way to transfer the marijuana from us to them. They couldn't agree on the price to pay the informant who had piloted the plane, and to top it all off, they wanted only part of the 15,000 pounds instead of taking the full load as was agreed upon. They wanted us to piecemeal it to them. It was a disaster.

As a result, the 15,000 pounds of marijuana was seized but no one was arrested. I remember how that burned me up at the time. One of the cops that I met down the road soon after this investigation used to always say, "Kilograms of drugs, or pounds of drugs are like bullets in a war. You can always make more no matter how much is seized. What I want are the soldiers, the men...they can't be replaced." And that has always been in the back of my head my entire career. The drugs taken off the street was a good thing. Don't get me wrong. We needed that. But we needed the leaders, organizers, financiers, soldiers, couriers, brokers, and transporters arrested and put in jail for a very long time.

11
Swallower/Re-Swallower

A round this time, Greg and I sort of went our separate ways. There were no hard feelings or anything, and nothing major caused this. It was more a generational gap. I was a new agent, young and aggressive. And, as stated previously, Greg had been with a local police department for many years before he was a DEA agent. So, he preferred more long term, slower paced investigations – cases like money laundering investigations, historical conspiracies – cases that are slower moving and more methodical but still crucial to the DEA mission. But that just wasn't me, not at that point in my career anyway. Those investigations came later in my career.

Anyway, there was another agent in my group by the name of Sean Vereault. He was young like me and was in my academy class at Quantico, as well, so we knew each other well. Prior to the DEA, he was a U.S. Customs Inspector assigned to the Miami International Airport. And he still had a lot of contacts there. Back then the DEA and the U.S. Customs Service did not always get along, but they desperately needed one another to get the job done. Why was this? Well, at that time the U.S. Customs Service did not have United States Code (USC) Title 21 authority. The DEA did.

Title 21 allowed you to actually make a seizure and then continue the operation proactively in an attempt to move further up the chain of command in an organization or further infiltrate the organization. Again, kilograms of cocaine and pounds of marijuana were just bullets in the war to me. I wanted the soldiers. However, on the flip side, the U.S. Customs Service had all the contacts and intelligence inside the airport. They had airline employees, ramp workers, concession workers, and all kinds of other airport employees acting as informants for them. However, once an arrest and/or seizure was made at the airport, their investigation ended. It couldn't continue without the DEA. Only if they passed the investigation to us could we then take it out onto the street and further the investigation. For example, if someone was arrested with a kilogram of cocaine in a bag attempting to board an outbound flight and if he or she decided to cooperate and tell us where the kilogram of cocaine came from, we as DEA agents could then try to further investigate by initiating an investigation of that person. Although we needed one another, we seldom got along. Alpha male type stuff!

Now that you have a little background, I'll tell you a little story that I find comical now although it was pretty unsettling at the time. Back then it was pretty common for drug organizations in South and Central America to use couriers or "swallowers" or "mules" to ingest cocaine or hide it on their person or insert it in an orifice in order to smuggle cocaine and heroin into the U.S. These people would be paid somewhere around $5,000 a trip which to you and I isn't worth the risk at all, but to some of these people it was more money than they would see in a lifetime. The organization would pack balloons or condoms with cocaine or heroin, sometimes up to a kilogram at a time, which is 2.2 pounds. The balloons or condoms would be swallowed by the drug swallowers and then excreted in the individuals' feces after they had arrived at their desired location by aircraft. Obviously, this was often a suicide mission. If one of these balloons or condoms ruptured inside of their stomachs for whatever reason during the trip, it was almost a guaranteed death. These stories are common, but I'll tell you one that I was involved with.

My fellow agent, Sean, was contacted one night by a U.S. Customs agent assigned to Miami International Airport. They had arrested a drug swallower coming off an inbound flight from Bogota, Colombia. He stated that the individual who had been arrested was willing to cooperate and asked if we would be interested in coming to the airport and interviewing him. He was willing to give us the names of those who had given him the balloons to swallow in Bogota as well as those to whom he was supposed to give the cocaine once he passed the balloons. We jumped at the chance and met up with one another at Miami International Airport. We hooked up with Sean's U.S. Customs buddy who proceeded to lead us into their lockup facility at the airport. We did the normal introductions with the defendant – the usual – showing our badges and credentials and telling the defendant our names. After the niceties and introductions were finished, we started the interview. And, as we were taught in the academy, we did the whole "Tell us everything you know, from the time you met the person in Bogota until now." routine. The funny part of this story was not who gave him the cocaine in Bogota or who was receiving the cocaine here in Miami as I actually don't remember any of that. What I do remember, and is the reason I'm even telling this story, is the bizarre and actually incredibly sad story that the defendant told us regarding his flight from Bogota to Miami. Or, better yet, the no flight part of the trip. Let me explain.

The defendant stated that he was dropped off at El Dorado International Airport in Bogota by one of the traffickers, but the flight he was supposed to take was literally minutes from departure. I'm not sure if the reason was because of the heavy traffic or that the defendant was picked up late, or that the defendant was just unprepared and lackadaisical. In any case, the flight was about to leave. That's all I remember. And he missed the flight. The next direct flight to Miami was literally hours away. To my horror, the defendant went on to explain that during the long wait he had to go to the bathroom, and I'm talking number two here. I remember sitting there as he explained that he waited as long as he possibly could, but he simply couldn't hold it and rushed to the bathroom. Obviously, he passed the balloons while on the toilet. And then the kicker. Not knowing what else to do and panicking and realizing that he had thousands of dollars of cocaine with him, he proceeded to rinse the balloons off in the sink and then he **reswallowed them**! All I remember wondering, and yes, gross I know, was if they went down any smoother the second time! But as I said in the beginning of this story, these people are desperate for money and will do anything, **anything** (obviously!) for this money which, again, is more than they will make in a lifetime. And the drug traffickers know this and prey upon them because of this mere fact.

12
Hector Lord Investigation

I want to tell this next story because it was another case I worked with Sean, and also to introduce the concept of a controlled delivery (CD) which are very common in the DEA but can be very trying to work.

To begin, it is important to understand that we have a worldwide presence. We have offices all over the world. For the longest time we had 72 offices in 56 countries and some larger countries had two or sometimes even three offices. I'm sure that there are even more offices in more countries now as this was about 30 years ago. These offices are usually located in the U.S. Embassy or Consulate of the host country. A lot of people throughout my career have often asked me why we have these foreign offices if we are part of the federal government and, more specifically, the U.S. Department of Justice. I wondered that too when I first started as a new agent. And doing these types of cases, these controlled deliveries, provided part of the answer.

First, we have these offices for liaison purposes. We assist the local counterparts with their investigations if there is U.S. nexus and, in turn, they assist the U.S. with our investigations if there is a host country nexus. This may be a bit confusing so let me fast forward a little bit to try to explain this point. From 1999 to 2002, I was assigned to the Brussels, Belgium country office. I will go into more detail about this part of my career later, but I need to make a quick point. When I was in Belgium, the ecstasy craze hit. Ecstasy, or MDMA, is an amphetamine, a stimulant. It was popular with teenagers and young adults. The big thing back then was to go to a rave or an all-night dance party and take ecstasy. You would then be able to dance for hours, stay up for days on end, and have euphoric thoughts and feelings. But it was deadly and these teenagers and young adults were overdosing and dying from ecstasy at an alarming rate. As usual, the U.S. was the number one consumer of ecstasy. And, at the time, all of the labs that were making ecstasy were in Belgium and The Netherlands. The Belgian Gendarmerie (the DEA/FBI equivalent in Belgium) would conduct investigations involving certain organizations in Belgium that were sending thousands of ecstasy tablets to the U.S. They would ask me to get them intelligence information from a certain DEA office in the U.S. that would assist with their investigation.

In turn, various local DEA offices stateside ran investigations involving organizations that were supplied with ecstasy by sources of supply in Belgium. The DEA offices in the U.S. would then task me to get them intelligence information from the Belgian Gendarmerie that would assist them with their investigations. It was all about information sharing. So, I was, in essence, a liaison officer working for my home agency, DEA, and my host government, in this case Belgium, at the same time. In other words, I was a middleman, an intelligence broker.

The other primary responsibility of a foreign assignment was to be more proactive. It was assisting in controlled delivery operations which was what I was referring to at the beginning of this story. What usually happened was that an arrest and seizure was made in the foreign country. In the Hector Lord case it started with an arrest in Colombia and a seizure of 1.2 kilograms of heroin. The individual arrested was a man by the name of Julio Dante who was willing to cooperate with the Colombian National Police (CNP) to help himself get a more lenient prison sentence. Dante told the CNP that he had a telephone number that he was supposed to call after he had arrived in Miami, and that person was supposed to take receipt of the drugs. The telephone number had been given to Dante by one of members of the organization. As usual, Dante was just a courier, kind of like a swallower mentioned previously, but Dante had the heroin sewn into the side of his travel bag, another very common smuggling method. But I need to digress.

Here I am (on the right) with Special Agent Sean Vereault after seizing 1.2 kilograms of Heroin in the Lord investigation.

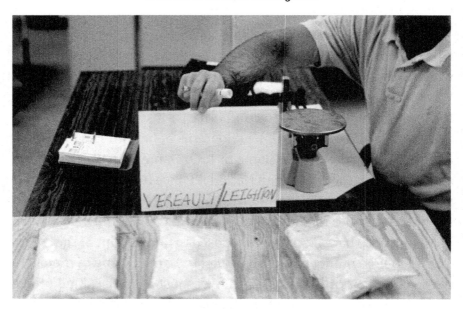

1.2 kilograms of Heroin

I need to take a moment here to mention something. Drug trafficking organizations will do **anything** to get their drugs into the U.S. Not almost anything but **anything**. It's all about the money, the Benjamins. It's greed, pure and simple. The organizations will use swallowers. We already spoke about those. They will use the courier's body cavities – vaginas and rectums – to conceal drugs. They will take a drug like cocaine and then turn it into liquid cocaine and then pour it into the fabric of clothes. Then when the cocaine arrives at its destination, the process is reversed in a lab to extract the cocaine. Hell, I've even seen an organization use a dog. **Please stop reading if you're an animal lover.** The organization actually sewed a kilogram of cocaine into the dog's fur. I actually saw the dog one time when working at Miami International Airport. The poor thing was half dead. Disgusting. That's the one thing I learned very quickly. Most of the scum I dealt with, investigated and arrested were vermin concerned with one thing and one thing only – **money**.

Back to the story. In February of 1993, Dante, escorted by two DEA agents from the Bogota Office, arrived in Miami. Sean and I met them at the airport and drove them back to our office. Once there, we had a meeting to decide the details of the operation. After tossing some ideas back and forth, we decided on an operational plan, which would be to rent a hotel room in Miami. We would have Dante in the room with a suitcase in which the heroin was concealed. We would have an adjoining room at the hotel with a couple agents staged inside. They would be there for Dante's security. They would also be monitoring a hidden camera/recorder that was concealed inside Dante's room. The recorder would be able to record both audio and visual. We would then have the rest of the agents in the group in their cars spread out around the hotel parking lot and in nearby streets. Dante would make the call to the number he was given and then the person who was supposed to take delivery of the heroin would arrive and we would arrest him that night. Simple, right? Wrong. So wrong.

When dealing with kilogram quantity drug traffickers, you

have to remember that they were usually more sophisticated, more business-like, more intelligent and more patient than your average street dealer. It was much different than buying rocks of crack from Johnny Greensneakers or from Joe Shit the Ragman at the intersection of Walk and Don't Walk. They usually spent time in prison and used their time in jail wisely by talking to other inmates about how they got arrested. They learned how law enforcement worked, how law enforcement operated, the methods we used in our investigations, and the equipment we utilized. And that was not good for us.

In this case we had Dante call the telephone number that he had been given. The person on the other end did not give a name. He simply asked where Dante was at the moment. So, Dante told him. The person then told Dante to stay there. Now we were committed. The rest of the night went by. Then the next day. Nothing. We had Dante call back a couple times the next day, but now no one answered. We were running on fumes. The agents in the group had been up for 24 hours with no end in sight. We had to start sending some agents home to get some sleep just in case it went through the next night. We even had Dante call back to Bogota asking what to do. He was told to wait. Dante was told to just sit in the hotel room and watch TV. Little did they know that there were ten DEA agents also there going on 24 hours without sleep and who hadn't seen their families for a couple of days. They knew what they were doing. They were waiting us out. They knew that agents and cops enjoyed their work but most of them had families. And they needed sleep like everyone else. They wouldn't and couldn't go day after day watching the hotel. The organization was going to wait us out!

Since we couldn't leave Dante alone with the heroin, and we didn't want to pull the plug to end the operation, we just had to wait. We ran a skeleton crew while we switched out people to go home, get some rest, kiss their families, and then head back in. Finally, after three days, there was a knock at Dante's door. The agents on surveillance outside were put on alert. The camera and recorder were activated. It was on! The strange thing is that the individual who had arrived and was meeting with Dante was very well dressed. He looked like a businessman. He just didn't look like a typical doper but, then again, you never can tell. Anyway, the individual and Dante engaged in some idle chit chat. One of the agents in the adjoining room was a native Spanish speaker and he was whispering into a DEA radio advising the other agents what was transpiring. Finally, after all this time, the individual grabbed the suitcase, said his goodbyes to Dante, shook Dante's hand and walked out of the room. He was immediately arrested as he walked through the parking lot. Finally.

Like every single drug dealer ever arrested, the individual who had taken possession of the suitcase swore up and down that he had been framed and that he had no idea what was inside the suitcase. This was all while we were booking him and processing him back at our office. This individual was Hector Lord and said he was an architect and that he had a family. He said that he had no reason to sell heroin, that he was very well-off and didn't need the money. Lord stated he had been asked by a friend to pick it up. When Lord was asked if he had inquired about what he was picking up, Lord stated no and that he trusted his friend. When asked who this person was, Lord refused to give us the name. He said he was afraid for his safety and for that of his family. But he swore he was innocent.

Well, Lord never wavered from his story and the case eventually went to trial. We had a pretty decent case against Lord since we did have a recorded conversation from that night at the hotel between Dante and Lord discussing the contents of the suitcase. You have to understand that although no one ever comes out and refers to it as heroin in any undercover meeting, it's pretty obvious what they are talking about even with coded words. When words like junk, smack, "H" and horse are used, it's pretty obvious that something illegal is happening. But as luck would have it, Lord survived to live another day. I'm not sure if it was his high-priced defense attorney, his polished manners and nice suits, or his family sitting right behind him, but the jury couldn't all agree on a verdict and the judge had no other option than to declare a hung jury and release Lord. I was devastated as that was my first trial! Thank God the U.S. Attorney's Office in Miami was very aggressive and decided to re-charge Lord but on lesser charges since the double jeopardy clause doesn't allow you to prosecute the same individual for the same crime twice, in this case after a hung jury. Fortunately, justice prevailed this time, and Lord was found guilty.

One funny side story about that trial. I couldn't remember if it was in the first trial or the re-trial, but Lord had hired a female defense attorney who was in private practice and very high priced. The Judge was Shelby Highsmith who ran his courtroom like a military platoon which was not a coincidence since he served in the U.S. Army from 1949 to 1955. Anyway, Judge Highsmith either sustained a motion or overruled a motion, which went against whatever objection this attorney made. She was not happy about it at all and let the judge know about it. However, he held his ground and then called for a brief recess to give the jury a break. Many people who weren't familiar with courtroom procedures didn't know that a federal courtroom had microphones placed throughout the room and that the judge's chambers had a speaker in which he or she could hear everything that was going on in the courtroom. This attorney must not have. So, as the brief recess began, the attorney heard the judge's chamber door close, and since she believed that the judge was out of ear shot, she whispered quietly, "What an asshole." The door of the judge's chambers opened up and Judge Highsmith came walking back to the bench. He was madder than a wet hen and **blasted** the attorney. He eventually ended his tirade and held her in contempt of court which I learned later carried with it a pretty hefty fine. Ah, I love the drama!

13
Testifying in Federal Court

"You show me someone who has never lost a case, and I'll show you somebody who has never tried a tough case."
– Assistant United States Attorney Guy Lewis.

Around this time, I met a prosecutor at the U.S. Attorney's Office in Miami. He was young and aggressive and a legal genius. His name was Guy Lewis. And, as previously stated, he had been one of the prosecutors in the Noriega trial. At the time, he was only about 32 years old. After the Noriega trial, Guy could have gone anywhere he wanted and had any plum assignment. But he wanted to stay on the front lines and prosecute cases. He was a soldier, too. That's how I met Guy. He taught me so much about testifying and the federal court system.

He loved court. He loved trials. He loved the pomp and circumstance. He loved the history of it all and honoring the U.S. Constitution. Don't get me wrong. He was a very fair prosecutor. When we made arrests, Guy would always offer the individuals a fair plea deal. But if they didn't take it then we would proceed to go to trial. And we won every trial we had together. The only blip on the radar screen was the Lord trial, the first one mentioned, which ended up in a hung jury. I remember being devastated after that. I didn't understand what had happened. But I remember Guy trying to cheer me up after and saying, "You show me someone who has never lost a case and I'll show you somebody who has never tried a tough case." I always remember that. It's so true. You can't just plead away the case because they are too tough or too daunting. You have to proceed because it's the right thing to do. Period.

So, like Guy, I learned to love trials. Sometimes after our court hearing had finished, I would sit in the back of the courtroom and stay and watch the rest of the docket. What I loved about it most was that it was the supreme test of justice. We put our evidence on; the defense put their evidence on. We called our witnesses; they called their witnesses. It always struck a primitive part of me that I honestly believe is in every man. It's mano a mano – man vs. man. And I have known a lot of agents who hate to testify, who hate trials. Period. And I never understood that. That's what it all comes down to. It was our time to shine and present our case to the jury. For days, weeks, and sometimes months we sat in cars on surveillance. We ate horrible food while on surveillance. We missed out on family time. We wrote a ton of reports in our cars. We risked our lives chasing around dangerous people. And now after the bad guy had been arrested and was sitting at the defense table while their attorney was calling you a liar or not totally truthful, we had an opportunity to go and get up on that stand and put our evidence on, look the jury in their eyes and tell them the story – the truth, the whole truth and nothing but the truth. There's no better system of justice in the world.

Speaking of that, there is an art to testifying. The beauty of it is to let it come to you. Let the prosecutor do all of the questioning, just follow their lead and answer their questions. What I mean by this is that when I was a young agent, I would get flustered on the stand sometimes. Everyone does. The defense attorney would be ripping me apart on the stand and Guy would just be sitting there at the prosecution table taking notes. Sometimes I wondered if he was even paying attention. But he would always rescue me on re-direct examination. He would always tell me to just answer their questions calmly and truthfully. Don't play their games as it's exactly what they want you to do – for you to get flustered in front of the jury.

Let me give you an example:

Defense Attorney: What's your name and title?

Me: Keith Leighton and I'm a Special Agent with the Drug Enforcement Administration, the DEA.

Defense Attorney: A what? Did I hear that right? A **Special** Agent? What makes you so **special**?

Me: Um, what? Excuse me? (*stammering*)

(*Defense Attorney would then finish his cross examination.*)

Guy on Re-Direct Examination: Agent Leighton who gave you that title 'Special Agent'?

Me: The DEA did. It's just the title they gave me. At the academy in Quantico, Virginia.

Guy: No further questions, your honor.

Simple stuff like that. Answer the question. Don't spar with them.

Another example was when I had to testify at a suppression hearing. A suppression hearing was when the defense counsel did exactly what it sounded like – they tried to suppress your evidence from being admitted into court for a number of various reasons. It was usually something to do with the custody of evidence or an unlawful search and seizure or something similar. In this case, it was actually police brutality, or excessive use of force or unnecessary roughness by the arresting officers.

It all started when I was assisting one of the other agents in the office with an arrest. Now, remember this was Miami in the early 1990s. And we were always taught at the academy to treat every subject like the other. It didn't matter if we were arresting a male or female or juvenile or someone in their 60s. They were all the same, and they all posed as risks until they were in handcuffs. If we let our guard down because we were arresting a female instead of a male, that was when people got hurt.

We ended up making this arrest and the subject was a female. I forget the exact scenario, but she was on foot and had reached her vehicle by the time the arrest team had moved in. And the vehicle happened to be an SUV. That was an even bigger danger because now she was behind the wheel of a potential weapon – her car – if she attempted to flee and run over an agent. I was part of this arrest team and on high alert with the car being in play. I was approaching the female from the front of the car while other agents were surrounding it, as well. I was yelling out all my normal arrest commands, both in English and Spanish, "Hands Up, let me see your hands, Manos arriba," over and over as I was getting closer and closer to the car door. I remember being very nervous as I approached because I couldn't see her hands. I finally got to the door and she was still just sitting there, but I still couldn't see her hands. So, I pulled on the door handle and thank God it was open. I proceeded to open the car door and grab the female by her shoulder and pull her out of the vehicle and to the ground.

It was the exact way we were taught at the academy when making an arrest. Get them to the ground as quickly as possible and get the handcuffs on them. Again, remember our clientele. We arrested drug dealers, not counterfeiters or shoplifters or j-walkers. And drug dealers were very often armed, especially in Miami. Anyway, she went down to the pavement and was cuffed. It should have been the end of story, but because it was an SUV and the seats were up a little higher than in a regular passenger car, she ended up getting a few scrapes when she landed. That's what led to the suppression hearing – they thought my arrest technique was too aggressive and overbearing.

We got into court with Guy being the prosecutor. This was early in my career, and I was still new to testifying. I learned another lesson about simply answering the defense counsel's questions and not getting riled up if they tried to jam you up. Just let the prosecutor rescue you on re-direct examination. So, I was on the stand and the brief exchange went something like this:

Defense Counsel (DC): Agent Leighton, how tall are you and what do you weigh?

Me: I'm 5'9 and about 180 pounds.

DC: And how about my client?

Me: Oh, I guess about five feet even and about 100 pounds.

DC: So, Agent Leighton, don't you think the force you used to extract my client from her vehicle was a bit excessive?

Me: Well, she could have shot me just like anyone else could have! A female can pull the trigger of a gun just like a man can!

As I stated that, out of the corner of my eye, I saw Guy's head just drop as he sat at the prosecution table. He was shaking his head back and forth. And, right then, I knew I had screwed up. I didn't just simply and calmly answer the question no matter how absurd. I had let them get under my skin once again. I had my emotions come into play which was always a no- no in court and when testifying.

As cool as can be, Guy asked me one question during re-direct examination which got everything back on track. It was this one question:

Guy: Agent Leighton, what were you taught at the DEA Academy as far as making an arrest of a drug dealer who has committed a felony and looking at a possible lengthy jail sentence?

Me: To get them on the ground as quickly as possible so that you have control of them and to get the handcuffs on them as quickly as possible regardless of their sex. We were taught to get them in control as soon as possible.

Guy: Nothing further, your honor.

That was it! Amazing! He taught me so much about testifying. I still remember it to this day and constantly told my younger agents the same thing. I told them these stories constantly hoping they didn't make the same mistakes that I did. And, at the end of the hearing, the judge ruled against the suppression of evidence and the defense counsel's motion. Eventually the female pled guilty to the charges and off to jail she went

I always remember when I first started working with Guy. Guy was a staunch conservative and only wore conservative suits, only black, navy blue, and charcoal gray ones. The shirt was either a starched white shirt or occasionally a light blue one always finished off with a repp (striped) tie. Even the cuffs of his pants had to be an inch and a half, no longer, no shorter. One day, we were meeting in his office before going over to the courthouse for some kind of hearing, and I walked into his office wearing a double-breasted suit. I thought he was going to have a heart attack. He almost lost his mind. He proceeded to give me a lecture about how I looked like either a defense attorney, or a used car salesman, or an insurance salesman and to never to wear that kind of suit to court. He was not happy with me. A few months later we had another court hearing of some kind and, as usual, we agreed to meet in his office. I walked in wearing a charcoal *single-breasted* suit, white shirt, red and black striped rep tie, inch and a half cuffs and polished black shoes. He took one look at me, jumped out of his seat and yelled, "Now that's what I'm talking about!" So funny.

Speaking of being conservative, I have to include this other funny Guy story. We were right in the middle of trial in a case against two Sikh Nationals that we had arrested – an individual by the name of Mo and another by the name of Ty. We had termed it Operation Blue Jay since these two individuals were from Toronto and the Toronto Blue Jays had just won the World Series that year. These two characters had been introduced to a TFO in my group, who was acting in an undercover capacity, by one of our informants. Supposedly, the informant and Mo had served time in prison together and had agreed to meet up after they had gotten out of prison to start working with one another again in the drug business.

Unfortunately for Mo, the informant had plans of his own and decided to work with the DEA instead after he was released from prison. These two Sikhs end up sending down three of their

BADGES, BAD GUYS & BUSTS

associates which I will refer to as Ken, Lou and Freddy to Miami to negotiate with the undercover agent for the purchase of cocaine. Ken, Lou and Freddy were supposed to buy this cocaine from the undercover agent and drive it back to Canada where it would be sold for a huge profit since cocaine in Miami was incredibly cheap compared to cocaine in Toronto. This was due to the fact that cocaine came from South America, just south of Miami, and a big mark up on price can lead to huge profits. It was the old buy low and sell high theory. Narcotics 101!

To make a long story short (the investigation took over a year), we ended up arresting Ken, Lou and Freddy. We seized $150,000 in cash which they had in their possession which was to be used to buy ten kilograms of cocaine. Ken and Freddy pled guilty almost immediately, but Lou decided to go to trial for whatever reason. After the trial had ended and Lou had been found guilty, the defense attorney for Lou asked Guy politely if we needed all of the items that we had taken from Lou at the time of his arrest. He was referring to items like a belt, car keys, loose change, his wallet, some miscellaneous cash, etc. It's not that we were going to seize these items but we had them since the day of the arrest since prisons don't take these items. They don't want the responsibility of keeping track of the items or maintaining/storing them. So, Guy said he didn't have a problem with it if I didn't. I didn't at all since I wanted to get rid of these items anyway. And, coincidently, I had brought the items with me as I was going to ask the defense attorney if I could turn them over to him anyway.

So, I pulled out the evidence bag containing all of these items, and the wallet came out. Guy asked me to hand him the wallet and said that he just wanted to go through it quickly to make sure that there wasn't anything of evidentiary value in it before we handed it over. All of a sudden Guy's face lit up as he pulled out a Republican National Party membership card. Guy was beaming and turned to Lou who was sitting at the defense table right next to the defense attorney. Now, you have to remember that Lou was just found guilty of attempting to purchase ten kilograms of cocaine. He also lost $150,000 cash to DEA asset seizure/forfeiture laws. And he was looking at about ten years of incarceration in a federal prison where he'd have to serve 80% of his time because there was no such thing as parole. Lou wasn't in the best of moods, obviously. Guy turned to him and said, "Lou, if I had known you were a member of the Republican National Party, we might have been able to work something out." No joke. I almost fell out of my seat laughing.

GUY STORY NUMBER TWO. I can't resist. After we had first arrested Ken, Lou and Freddy, Guy and I took a business trip to Detroit to get some background information on all three individuals. We had discovered during our investigation that both the Detroit, Michigan Police Department and the DEA office in Detroit knew Lou and Ken well and had arrested both of them at one point or another. We wanted to review the criminal files and investigative paperwork to prepare for trial. We did all that and it went fine. But on the way back to Miami, we stopped in Memphis, Tennessee for a couple of days so that we could interview a prisoner who was incarcerated in Memphis at a Bureau of Prisons (BOP) facility relative to one of our other investigations. It was basically two separate business trips combined into one. Guy was from Memphis and went to law school there, so he knew the area pretty well so he proceeded to book us into a really nice, swanky, boujee hotel. We landed, checked in and we proceeded to go out to a nice dinner. At dinner Guy asked me if I wanted to work out in the morning since the hotel had a really nice gym. I said definitely as I always packed a set of workout gear in case the chance arose. It was a plan. We agreed to meet in the gym at 7:00 a.m. for an early morning workout before breakfast. Then we would travel out to the BOP facility to interview the prisoner.

It was 7:00 a.m. when Guy and I met in the gym for the workout. I asked him what he wanted to do first. Weights, a run, or some other cardio workout? He replied that we should jump in the sauna first to loosen up. I agreed. No biggie. It wasn't the way I normally start a workout, but whatever. It was what it was. We sat in there for a while and then got out. I then asked Guy what's next? He said that we should jump in the hot tub for a while to **really** get loose. Um...okay. So, we did that. Now, don't forget, we were supposed to workout, shower and meet for breakfast around 8:00 a.m. before we started our day. And it was already 7:30 a.m. by the time we got out of the hot tub. I was so perplexed about what we were going to do next. I remember thinking, *when is the damn workout going to start?* All I remember was being loose as a goose or more like a wet noodle at this point. Bracing myself for the answer, I asked Guy how he wanted to finish the workout. He said that a nice hot shower would really hit the spot. Of course. Why not? Just more hot water. I was about waterlogged by now so what did I care? We showered and then got dressed for the day. As we sat down for breakfast, I remember saying to Guy, "I have to ask you, what kind of workout was that? That was the strangest workout I've ever done. I mean, we didn't **do** anything. Not a thing."

He smiled and replied back in his thick southern drawl, "That's what's referred to as a gentleman's workout, my friend." So funny!

GUY STORY NUMBER THREE. As I stated previously, Guy was very conservative. As in most judicial districts around the U.S., some judges were conservative and some were liberal, all depending on which sitting U.S. President nominated them to the bench. Well, one federal judge in Miami at that time was Judge Lenore Nesbitt and she was **ultra** conservative. What more is that she **loved** Guy. One day we were in trial – it seemed as if we were always in trial those days – and Guy stood up to object and the conversation went like this:

Guy: Objection, Your Honor.

Judge Nesbitt: Sustained

Defense Counsel (*in absolute shock*): Your Honor? Seriously? How can you sustain it when you don't even know the objection? He never stated it.

Judge Nesbitt: Oh, yes, sorry. Mr. Lewis, what is the objection?

Guy: Asked and answered, Your Honor.

Judge Nesbitt: Sustained.

Defense Counsel: (*drops his head and returns to the defense table shaking his head.*)

GUY STORY NUMBER FOUR. And the last, I promise. Back then we had a really tight group. We all loved the job; we all worked very hard at it; we took our work seriously; we had pride and we all were diligent soldiers. And with Guy as our prosecutor, almost as if Group 9 had him on retainer, we were a force to be reckoned with. So, again, I found myself in a trial with Guy. I remember this case because the poor schmuck should have never gone to trial. I mean, we had a rock-solid case against him. We had a ton of incriminating evidence and the dude was guilty as sin. He didn't stand a chance. The only thing we didn't have was a signed confession. The trial proceeded as normal, and the closing arguments had just wrapped up. The judge then gave the jury their deliberation orders, explained them all nice and slow, and then released the jury to deliberate. As soon as the 12th juror had left the court room and entered the jury room and just as the door closed behind him, one of the courtroom security guards – bluecoats as we always referred to them – turned to Guy and me and asked, "They aren't back yet?" meaning the jury. Even he knew it was a slam dunk!

14
Ricky Alejandro Investigation

My partner at the time, Sean, had recently been re-assigned to the Bogota Office and was off attending Spanish language training in Washington, D.C. when a request for investigative assistance came in from our San Jose, Costa Rica country office and was received by my group. By this time the Miami office had conducted another personnel shift to make the groups as evenly as possible with a mix of junior and senior agents, especially since we had just lost Sean to language school and soon, he would be off to Bogota. Subsequently, an agent by the name of Rick Bendekovic was re-assigned from one of the other enforcement groups in Miami to the one to which I was assigned. Soon after that re-assignment, we started working together and during the next four years became very good friends. He's still a very close friend of mine, and we still keep in touch to talk about the old days.

During this time, the San Jose office informed us that they were assisting their local Costa Rican counterparts with a drug investigation in San Jose and had recently determined that the drugs, cocaine in this case, were being sent to an individual in Miami by the name of Ricky Alejandro. The local counterparts were up on a wiretap and had intercepted phone calls between their organization in Costa Rica and Alejandro where the transportation of multi-kilograms of cocaine from Costa Rica to Miami were being negotiated. We proceeded to initiate an investigation into the members of the Alejandro organization that were living and operating in Miami. It was a fairly quick investigation and within a day or two, one of the agents from the Costa Rica office traveled to Miami to attend a meeting between our office and the U.S. Attorney's Office. I was out of the country traveling and on vacation for a couple of weeks at the time, so I missed a lot of this investigation. By the time I had gotten back to work, we were ready to arrest Alejandro as the investigation was over. The reason I'm telling this story is actually the 'after' story. Since much of the evidence involving Alejandro was in the custody of the Costa Rican counterparts, such as the aforementioned intercepted phone calls involving Alejandro with the wiretap order, the prosecutor at the time decided that we needed to take a trip to Costa Rica to examine all of the evidence. After all, if Alejandro decided to go to trial, we would need to be familiar with what evidence was involved in the Costa Rican investigation. So, we were off. The three of us – Rick, the prosecutor, and me.

I remember the flight down to Costa Rica as if it were yesterday. Rick and I treated it like a kind of holiday since Costa Rica was a sovereign country and we were not allowed to carry our firearms with us. We had a blast, drinking and laughing the entire flight. I can also remember that this was about 1994 and that the airlines still allowed smoking on their flights. It's funny to think about smoking on an airplane these days. We landed in Costa Rica with no issues and were met at the airport by one of the agents assigned to the San Jose office. He took us to our hotel and let us get cleaned up and unpacked. He mentioned that a few of the counterparts, local Costa Rican cops that they worked with, wanted to meet us and take us out for a few drinks. We said sure and proceeded to get settled in our hotel room. The prosecutor we were with politely declined saying she had some work to catch up on.

Eventually we all met in the hotel lobby and were introduced to the Costa Rican cops. Between their poor English and our poor Spanish, we muddled through hellos and introductions the best that we could with a lot of sign language going on. We then proceeded to all pile into one of a couple of the Costa Rican police cars and then headed off to the bar.

When we got there, we ordered beers and sat down at the bar. Like all cops do, we traded war stories with the agent from the San

Jose office translating for all of us. About that time, I was getting a strange vibe that something was off. Like a sixth sense. Something didn't fit or feel right. The thing that I thought was odd was that I was getting hit on **constantly** by the most beautiful women while I was sitting at the bar. It was strange. My game was never that good! Anyway, I just shrugged it off, laughed and tried to enjoy myself. A little while later, I needed to go to the restroom. I politely excused myself and started walking to find the rest room. Then it hit me. There were no dudes but us in this place, only women. And there were **a lot** of them. And they were all staring at me the entire time. Suddenly, I realized that I was in a **brothel**! I had never ever been in one in my life and forgot that they were pretty common in countries in Central and South America. We got out of there in a hurry! So, that was one funny story about the trip. The other story, well, not so funny.

After a few days of work and examining the evidence, we were happy with the way everything had worked out. We felt that if Alejandro decided to go to trial, we would be ready. So, it was time to fly back to Miami. Rick and I were again laughing and drinking on the flight when all of a sudden, with only about an hour to go until we were scheduled to land in Miami, he got very quiet and pensive. I asked him if something was wrong a couple of times, but he shook it off saying it was nothing. As we got closer and closer to landing, I could tell his mood was getting worse. Then, all of a sudden, he broke it to me.

Right before we left Costa Rica and during the ride to the airport, Rick asked if I remembered that he was in the back seat with one of the Costa Rican cops while I was in the front seat. I told him that of course I remembered. I told him that I was there, and it was only a few hours ago. Rick proceeded to tell me that while I was talking to the driver of the car, the agent assigned to the San Jose office, and enjoying the scenery, the local Costa Rican cop in the back handed Rick a kilogram of cocaine to take back with him to Miami as evidence. The cop explained that it was one of the kilograms that they had seized during the investigation involving Alejandro, and perhaps we could use it for trial if needed. I was starting to sweat about then and did not want to hear where this story was going. This was going to end badly, I could tell. Rick continued. He was, at first, shocked. Then surprised. So, not wanting to insult the cop, he took the kilogram of cocaine and put it in his carry-on bag. Then he boarded the flight. You have to remember that this was the mid-1990s, way before 9-1-1. And there was no such thing as TSA. Additionally, we were flying out of an airport in Central America. Needless to say, no one examined the carry-on carried by Rick as we proceed to board the flight. It wouldn't have mattered anyway as we were escorted by the Cost Rican cops right up to our gate.

I remember thinking, *Oh shit, this isn't good. How are we going to pull this one off?* We had to clear U.S. Customs in Miami upon arrival and here we were with a brick of cocaine in our possession. Don't get me wrong. As described previously, this sort of stuff is done all of the time in controlled delivery investigations like the ones explained earlier in this book, such as the Lord story. That was when the agents from the Bogota office brought the heroin with them when they travelled from Colombia to Miami. But they needed a pass-through letter, which we didn't have, and in order to get one, it would take about two weeks of forms, prep work and approvals. We didn't have two weeks! We had about an hour. We didn't have the pass-through letter because we didn't know we were going to be coming back with some souvenirs for our families, a couple of cheesy trinkets bought at the airport gift shop for some of our co-workers back in Miami **and a kilo of cocaine!**

Our only option was to call U.S. Customs from the plane as soon as we were close to landing and had a cell signal. We did just that and just laid on the sword and pled *mea culpa*. We tried to explain what had happened which they found very hard to believe, but it was true. What else could we do or say? Well, pissed off or not, U.S. Customs had been informed, and they were just going to have to deal with it one way or another.

Before long, the plane landed and taxied to the jetway. I remember turning to Rick and asking what we do now. He responded that we should just remain in our seats and that U.S. Customs would either board the plane and retrieve us, or that there would be an announcement asking us to please come to the front of the plane. So, we sat and waited. And waited. And waited. We waited until everyone was off the plane, leaving us the only passengers remaining. We sat there until the flight attendants told us that we had to leave. Man, was that uncomfortable. What were we going to say or ask? Maybe we could say something like, "Can we please stay here because the minute we step off this plane we're going to get arrested?" So, we got up and walked off the plane hoping to see a couple of friendly U.S. Customs Agents waiting for us. We did not.

We had no choice but to proceed down the jet bridge. As we came out of the jet bridge and into the terminal, we did notice a couple of Customs agents standing over to the side of the terminal not really talking or paying too much attention, certainly not to us. We knew they were Customs agents without a doubt as federal agents were always able to pick one another out of a crowd. But they couldn't be there for us, could they? They didn't seem to have a care in the world, much less looking for two DEA agents with a kilo of cocaine in their possession. So, we decided to just keep walking since we did not want to interfere with some operation that they had going on. You never knew as Customs agents were always working and always busy in an airport like Miami International.

Within a few minutes we reached U.S. Immigration which was no big deal since we only had to show U.S. Passports. We did so and kept walking. Well, this is where the rubber hit the road. We had reached U.S. Customs. I had a feeling that this wasn't going to go as smoothly as clearing immigration. Just a hunch. I felt like I was going to pass out. My mouth was so dry, and I was having trouble swallowing. I was trying to do the math in my head of how much time I'd be serving and how old I'd be when I got out of jail. When the U.S. Customs Inspector asked if we had anything to declare, I almost burst out laughing from the absurdity of it all. Well, we asked to speak to a supervisor after identifying ourselves. And we explained that we were the DEA agents that had called from the air requesting assistance with a pass-through letter. Just about then the two Customs agents that we had seen a few minutes earlier showed up and started reading us the riot act and getting in our faces. We were chided and lectured. They then asked why we didn't see them and approach them. We tried to explain and told them that we had seen them, but we didn't want to ruin any operation that they had going. It didn't work. They were pissed.

The funny thing is how this story ended. We were eventually allowed to "pass-through" with our cocaine, and then we proceeded to go down to baggage claim to get our luggage. While we were waiting at the belt, one of the Customs agents who had just verbally accosted and attacked us came up to us with this big cheesy smile on his face and asked how the trip went and did we have fun. My partner, Rick, didn't play like that. He snapped and turned to the guy and said to get out of his face. Rick told the guy to fuck off since he had just humiliated us in front of a ton of people and for what? Rick just lit into the guy about how we didn't do anything wrong, about how we got the kilo and how unexpected it was and on and on and on. That poor guy took an ass whipping that day. Rick crushed him. I loved it. I worked with Rick for a few years, and he didn't take any shit from anyone. Needless to say, we had no other issues that day at the airport. We went home, mentally exhausted.

15
Freeport, Bahamas

A nother very interesting investigation that I worked in Miami started out simple enough. The thought that it would eventually lead me to Freeport, Bahamas never ever entered my mind. It started out like this.

My supervisor at the time had been assigned to the Ft. Lauderdale, Florida office for a time before being assigned as my supervisor in Group 9. But he still maintained close friendships with some of the local police officers that he worked with in Ft. Lauderdale while he was assigned there. One day he got a call from one of these friends who informed him that they had recently arrested an individual for drug trafficking in the Ft. Lauderdale area. This person wanted to cooperate to help himself out, but the only drug dealer he knew and could give up was living and operating in Freeport, Bahamas. And knowing that they were local cops and that their jurisdiction was the Ft. Lauderdale area and that the DEA had an office in Freeport, it was a no brainer to turn it over to us. So, my supervisor assigned the investigation to me.

The first thing I did was contact the Ft. Lauderdale officers to set up a time to meet one another, to listen to what information they had, and to discuss strategy. During this meeting, I was informed that the person they had arrested obtained his drugs, in this case cocaine, from an individual who would meet him on the ocean and basically do the transfer boat-to-boat since they both owned boats. The trip was approximately two hours and change, so they would simply meet halfway and make the exchange which posed a problem for us. We couldn't really run the same scenario for a number of reasons.

First, after the defendant had been arrested and went to federal court for his initial appearance, he had been released by the judge pending a trial but on strict reporting requirements. And we were sure that travelling out of the country wouldn't meet these requirements. Judges were funny like that as no judge wanted to be responsible for a fugitive. Also, it would be a hard situation to control as we would need to be present to witness everything and corroborate the transaction, as well, and control the defendant. Additionally, the defendant had mentioned to us that he would always pay for the cocaine up front, meaning that he had to come up with the cash beforehand. Then he would sell the cocaine at a slight mark-up and keep the profits. But he always had to make sure that he put aside whatever amount he needed for the next load of cocaine. And at about $25,000 a kilogram at that time, there was no way we were going to be able to front the defendant thousands and thousands of dollars. After much deliberation, we came up with a brilliant idea, or we thought we had.

Because it was a very large office, the Miami office had a radio room manned by a 24/7 dispatch crew. One of the local police officers at the meeting that day asked about this radio room and the range it had. I said I had no idea and asked what the officer was thinking. He said that maybe we could have the defendant set up a transaction just like normal but instead of being on his boat and meeting with the drug trafficker, he would be in the radio room calling out to the drug trafficker, asking if he was in route to the rendezvous point, his location, his coordinates, etc. Then we would just intercept the boat and make the drug seizure and arrests. It was a long shot but we really had no choice.

The drug trafficker was a salty old Bahamian sea captain who never left the Bahamian island chain, so it was a moot point to even see if we could lure him out of the Bahamas. Additionally, every transaction that the defendant and the Bahamian drug trafficker had done in the past went the exact same way. Consequently, if the scenario were suddenly changed, he would most likely smell a rat. Drug dealers are notoriously rigid and strict when it comes to their routines. And very suspicious if it's changed! It's a defense mechanism and how they survive without going to jail.

The next step was to contact the DEA office in Freeport to request their assistance as they were the closest office to the area in the Atlantic Ocean where the defendant and the Bahamian drug trafficker usually met in the past and completed their drug deals. The agent that I contacted was an individual by the name of Stephen Luzinski. He was very accommodating and said that he would do whatever was needed to assist. It was then agreed that we would fly over to have a meeting to work out the logistics and complete an operational plan. The two local police officers that I was working with and I were on a plane a few days later. It wasn't a good sign to me when, during the short plane ride over to Freeport, we hit an air pocket or something and proceeded to drop for what felt like 50 feet, right out of the blue.

We eventually landed at the airport in Freeport all in one piece. We cleared Immigration and Customs, jumped in a cab and headed off to the hotel. Steve told us that he would meet us there. Not long after we checked in and were settled in the hotel, Steve showed up. We really hit it off well, especially since Steve, who was a former Ft. Lauderdale cop before becoming a DEA agent, and the two local police officers that were with me knew all the same people. That was a nice ice breaker.

We then proceeded to meet over the next two days and slowly hashed out a game plan. Our defendant would contact the Bahamian drug trafficker and set up a cocaine transaction. We knew from our defendant's debriefings that their transactions were usually in the 20-kilogram range, so we decided to keep it the same. We figured if the defendant were to up the order suddenly after all the previous transactions, it would raise a flag with the Bahamian drug trafficker. And, as I mentioned above, we would have the defendant in the radio room calling out to the Bahamian on the radio. When he was spotted, his vessel would be stopped and boarded. When I asked who would be doing this, Steve smiled and said to leave that up to him. He stated that they would use their number one asset, the U.S. Coast Guard to assist. WOW! The U.S. Coast Guard! We ended our meetings and went to work.

Soon after our arrival back in Miami we had the plan in place. Our defendant decided to meet the Bahamian drug trafficker and complete the 20-kilogram cocaine transaction on a certain date. We would have the defendant in the radio room trying to reach the Bahamian on the radio to try to lure him out into international waters. The two police officers who I was working with would be with him to monitor what he was saying on the radio. I, in turn, would fly back over to Freeport and hook up with Steve and assist with the interdiction of the vessel.

The big day finally came. I remember flying out of Miami on a small puddle jumper. It was called something like Island Air or Tropic Air. I remember walking out on the tarmac to board the plane on a blistering hot summer day. A baggage handler loading luggage from a baggage cart onto the plane was sweating profusely. I boarded, found my seat, and tried to make myself as comfortable as I could on an eight-seat plane. I then watched in horror as that same worker I had just watched load the bags proceed to close the luggage door below the plane, walk up inside the cockpit and settle down behind the controls. I remember thinking, *That's the pilot? Someone please get him a glass of water...and a cold compress! Good Lord!*

We made the 20-minute flight with no problems. Once again, Steve met me at the Freeport airport. He took me to the hotel and dropped me off, and we called it a night.

The next day came and proved to be quite long. We started with a big briefing about the day's operation. We, of course, were there along with local Freeport police officers and the U.S. Coast Guard. The plan was to have the defendant in Miami reach out for the Bahamian drug trafficker as if he was en route to meet him. We would then track the vessel that he was on and then make an interdiction stop when we felt it appropriate. Simple, right? Wrong again. We eventually boarded the U.S. Coast Guard cutter and set off.

We knew the approximate coordinates of where the defendant and the Bahamian were supposed to meet, so we set off for that area. There were two very pleasant things that I experienced on the U.S. Coast Guard cutter right away. The first was that although I was a civilian with only about four years on with the DEA at that point, and they were in the military, I outranked almost everyone on the cutter except for the Commanding Officer (CO) and the Executive Officer (XO). Everywhere I went and everyone I spoke to always referred to me as "sir." I thought that was kind of cool. The other thing that really impressed me was their enthusiasm and willingness to help. They were really into the mission. I guess one of the reasons, as told to me by one of the crew members, was that it got incredibly boring just "poking holes in the ocean" as he put it meaning just going back in forth or in circles waiting for a call for assistance or something to investigate. That was nice to hear.

Soon after the mission started, we had our first hiccup. The radio system was not powerful enough to reach the area of the ocean that was supposed to be the meeting point. The defendant tried over and over, but the transmissions couldn't be received. We were screwed. Now what? By this time, we had located what we thought was the Bahamian vessel. At least we were pretty sure based on the description of the vessel from the defendant and the coordinates in which the vessel was positioned at that moment.

So, the only thing to do at this point was to track it via radar while staying in the area but also out of sight. A U.S. Coast Guard cutter is a very large vessel and can be spotted a long way away, especially with the bright colors of the U.S. Coast Guard vessels. And every maritime smuggler knew the outline of a U.S. Coast Guard cutter on the horizon. Its red and white design was unmistakable. So, we had to be careful and just wait him out. Obviously, we were worried that he would give up on our defendant, but for right now he was just idling and waiting.

In the meantime, another nice little perk was that there was a galley (kitchen) and a U.S. Coast Guard crewmember who was the cook. He made us all a delicious lunch. Another really cool thing I learned while aboard the cutter that day was that every crewmember had a very specific job that he/she was responsible for. And throughout the day, the crew would check levels, gauges, instruments, etc. every hour on the hour and record the results. Whether it was fuel, electronics, food, clean water, motor/engine elements or any other tasks, they were all monitored constantly. It was a very efficient operation. We waited. And waited.

Another problem arose – it was starting to get dark. This meant that we had to stay even farther away from the Bahamian vessel so it didn't see our running and safety lights. Speaking of lights, here is another funny little story. Right around this time I was up on the bridge with the CO and XO just asking questions, telling stories, getting to know one another and killing time. And it was pitch black except for the glow of all of the instruments. I remember asking why they didn't keep all of the lights on in the bridge while they traveled. This turned out to be a very dumb question. The CO proceeded to turn on the lights and asked me to look outside. I did and couldn't see anything but my reflection. He explained that whenever anyone travels at night, whether it's in a car, plane, or boat, the only way to see outside at night is to keep the lights off. Oof! That was an embarrassing moment.

Just at that time, we received word that the Bahamian vessel had fired up its engines and was moving at a pretty good clip back towards Freeport. We immediately made a command decision to follow it and interdict it. It was our only shot at that point as the Bahamian trafficker must have given up on our defendant. One of the issues that concerned us at that point was that the U.S. Coast Guard had the authority to board any vessel that was either in international waters or in U.S. territorial waters but not in another country's waters. And it was moving fast back towards Bahamian waters. I remember turning to the XO at that point who was actually operating the cutter and asking if the Bahamian was going to be able to outrun us since we were about a mile away from him. He just looked at me, smiled and stated, "No, that's not happening. There's no chance of that." And we roared off in pursuit through the black Atlantic Ocean. That was an amazing feeling. Talk about an adrenaline rush! And the XO was so right. We flew in that cutter through the black night. We made up incredible time, and within minutes the Bahamian boat was in sight. At that point a decision was made to stop the cutter since we were getting very close to the vessel. Additionally, the cutter was so big and its wake so powerful that it could easily tip over a lot of other smaller vessels.

So, we made the decision to load up and launch the surf boat or inflatable boat, basically a large raft that all cutters carry to get closer to other vessels. A few U.S. Coast Guard personnel jumped in and proceeded to ask me if I wanted to go. There was no way I was passing this up and responded with an enthusiastic "Hell, yes!" Then it got kind of comical. For starters, all of these surf boats and rafts have a mounted machine gun turret in the middle of the raft. And all of the crew on the surf boat/raft each carried an M4 machine gun. And there I was with a Smith and Wesson Model 60 snub nose 5-shot revolver. Like that was going to make a difference! (For clarification, Steve loaned it too me earlier that day while we were still on shore. He knew I couldn't bring my DEA issued firearm to a foreign country so he loaned me his back-up weapon to me for protection).

We eventually arrived in the area of the Bahamian vessel. Thankfully, the Bahamians knew who they were dealing with and stopped right away. There was no chase. At first, they did try to outrun us but we were on top of them in no time. So, they stopped. They didn't want any trouble with us. We boarded the vessel and explained to the crew who we were and what we were doing. We proceeded to ask permission to search the boat, and it was granted. They actually gave us no problems whatsoever. After a lengthy search we found and seized 18 kilograms of cocaine. Now we had to figure out how to get the vessel and crew back to Freeport since the decision had been made to arrest all of the crew members onboard for trafficking cocaine. We knew the vessel could never outrun us so we made the decision to just follow it back to Freeport as it operated under its own power. Besides, we had the cocaine in our possession.

If the day hadn't been long enough already, it was going to get a lot longer. The vessel's engines, using every possible amount of power to outrun us, at first anyway, had overheated and shut down and wouldn't fire back up! What a sickening feeling! I had been up at dawn, on the ocean all day, and all I wanted to do was get my feet on dry land. The only option at this point was to tow the vessel back to Freeport ourselves. This literally took hours. Actually, not hours but the rest of the night. We didn't arrive back at Freeport until dawn. But what an adventure!

That's Steve Luzinski on the left and I am kneeling next to him. The other two individuals are with the Bahamian Drug Enforcement Unit (DEU) and the DEA Freeport, Bahamas office, respectively. In front of us are the 18 kilograms of Cocaine that we seized in the Bahamas.

16
The Antoine Walker Investigation

*"Kid, if you don't get sued at least once in your career you aren't
doing your job right."*
— Charlie Cecil (deceased), Senior DEA Agent,
Miami Field Division

In this investigation, Guy Lewis from the U.S. Attorney's Office
had contacted me one day to see if I wanted to assist him in
adopting an investigation. First, let me explain what an adoption
is. The federal system had certain guidelines as to the amount of
drugs needed for federal prosecution. In Miami, that amount was
five kilograms. But these guidelines were different in every part of
the country. For example, someone would need a lot less cocaine in
Duluth, Minnesota for federal prosecution than in Miami. If a state
or local agency initiated an investigation and for whatever reason
ended up seizing more than the federal threshold, it could petition
the US Attorney's Office to take the prosecution instead of the State
Attorney's Office.

The main reason for this was that criminals typically served
much longer sentences in the federal system. And there was no such
thing as parole like there was in many state systems. So, taking
cases federally was always the preferred method. As a result, the
U.S. Attorney's Office would typically take the investigation if the
Assistant United States Attorney, in this case Guy Lewis, felt that it
was a strong case. And he did. In doing so, he contacted me to guide
the state/local officers, in this case local officers assigned to the

North Miami Beach Police Department, through the complex federal court system which was a completely different animal than the state court system. We inherited the Antoine Walker investigation through adoption. One other side note: In an adoption case the proactive investigation had usually already been completed, the targets had been arrested and all that was left was the judicial part. Because of that, it was basically an assignment in which we were primarily assisting the prosecutor prepare the case for trial

I met with the arresting officers to get a full outline of their investigation so I could have some background knowledge. That was pretty basic and took place a day after Guy had called me asking about the adoption. It was a pretty typical case. It was a ten-kilogram cocaine buy-bust operation. Again, meaning an informant or an undercover agent met with the target, bought the ten kilograms of cocaine, and the target was then arrested or busted, hence a buy-bust as was described earlier in the book. In this case, it was an undercover agent who worked for the North Miami Beach Police Department.

The transaction took place just as planned. The meeting took place in a strip mall parking lot. When the undercover agent asked the target, Antoine Walker, to see the cocaine, Walker walked the officer over to a car and showed him the cocaine, either in the trunk or in a duffel bag in the car or something similar. The undercover agent said that it looked okay and that he had to grab the money from his car and would be right back. As the undercover agent was walking to the vehicle, he gave either a visual arrest signal or a verbal arrest signal to the arrest team stationed throughout the parking lot. The arrest team moved in and made the arrest without any issues or problems.

However, in this case there was a bit of an issue, one that we commonly saw in our investigations. It was referred to as counter surveillance. And it meant exactly what it sounded like – surveillance counter or against our surveillance. They, the bad guys, were looking for us just as we were looking for them. In other words, the target in this case, Antoine Walker, brought along counter surveillance that day in the parking lot acting as a lookout for him. A few of the arresting officers stationed around that parking lot had seen a car circling the lot and noticed that the driver was staring at Walker and Walker's vehicle as if keeping an eye out for him, making sure he was safe and not ripped off. This individual wouldn't take his eyes off Walker. Anyway, one of the more seasoned officers out there that day on the arrest team, being aware of the danger of this, quickly grabbed a couple of other officers and stopped this car and questioned the driver. The driver proceeded to make up some kind of story about meeting a lady friend of his there to meet up and go shopping. Of course, they couldn't really prove what their suspicions were and it was not against the law to cruise around a parking lot at a strip mall looking for your lady friend.

As a result, there was nothing that could be done at the time other than to make sure the undercover agent was safe the entire time. Then, one of the officers asked the driver of this vehicle to provide some kind of identification. This person proceeded to hand over his driver's license to the officer. The officer quickly checked with his dispatcher back in the radio room of the North Miami Police Department to determine if there were any wants or warrants out for this individual. There weren't. The officer then asked the dispatcher if the individual had any type of criminal history. The officer was informed that this person didn't have an arrest record. He had no choice but to write down all of the pertinent information from the driver's license and let the individual go. Of course, when the Walker was arrested, the officers tried to locate this person, but he was nowhere to be found. He was long gone.

It was at this point of the investigation that the officers brought the investigation to the U.S. Attorney's Office, specifically Guy Lewis, since they knew that they had seized more than enough cocaine from Walker to meet the federal guidelines for federal prosecution. And it was at this time that Guy contacted me to set up a meeting with the officers as mentioned earlier. The investigation proceeded as usual with the normal court appearance that one would find in the federal court system – the initial appearance, the pre-trial detention hearing, the probable cause hearing and arraignment, the discovery process, etc. Eventually, Walker decided to plead guilty. It was a smart move as he was looking at a lot of time. As a part of most plea agreements, there is usually a requirement for the defendant, in this case Walker, to meet with investigators and tell them everything he knows about the day of the arrest, the role of everyone involved in the transaction, and the organization behind the crime. It's called a proffer. The same held true in this investigation.

A proffer was scheduled in which Walker was going to meet with the officers and tell them everything that he knew about this crime. The day of the proffer came, but I couldn't remember if the defendant volunteered this information or if one of officers in attendance asked it of Walker. However, it was revealed that the individual in the car that day circling the strip mall lot **was** counter surveillance and was involved in the transaction that day. Walker admitted that it was his brother. Since that officer on scene that day had taken down all the information from the driver's license presented to him by the driver of the vehicle, Walker's brother could be included in the overall conspiracy and charged in the crime. That's exactly what was done.

After the proffer had been completed, the officers took the information from the driver's license, completed an affidavit and presented it to Guy for review. Knowing that a federal agent would have to swear this warrant out in front of a federal judge, it was at this point that Guy contacted me to get involved in this investigation, and it was at this point that I first met the North Miami Beach Police officers as described earlier in this story. After meeting with them, I took the affidavit to a federal judge and swore it out before him requesting that an arrest warrant be granted for this person. The judge signed it and the arrest warrant was granted. As stated previously, this was an interesting twist since adoptions don't usually turn proactive, but this one did. There was another arrest to be made which was exciting to me since it was totally unexpected. It was a very rewarding feeling to be able to take an investigation that was basically done when it was handed off to me and then be able to take it a step further and make it just a little bit better than when I received it. I was excited at the moment, but it wasn't going to be all roses.

When we got an arrest warrant, we usually started with the basics to try to find our target. In this case, I went to one of the intelligence analysts assigned to the Miami office and asked her to run the name through all of her databases and indices, basically property searches, real estate searches, employment history, marriage records, department of motor vehicles and what not. We obtained a few leads through these searches, but we couldn't find our target. We spent weeks looking for him to no avail. There was only so much time we could spend on one case. Miami was a very busy place. There were other cases that needed to be worked, and the officers and agents assisting us had their own cases to work. Basically, and this was just human nature, everyone started losing interest and started getting frustrated.

So, it was time to turn the arrest warrant over to the U.S. Marshals Service. This branch of the federal government is responsible for finding federal fugitives and then arresting them once they have been found. They are the best at it. And our Memo of Understanding (MOU) with the U.S. Marshal's Service, just like a lot of other federal agencies, stated that after a certain period of time if the individual could not be located, we (DEA) were required to relinquish the arrest warrant to the U.S. Marshal's Service. And that's exactly what was done. And then it got **really** interesting.

One day sometime after turning the arrest warrant over to the U.S. Marshal's Service, I received a phone call from a particular U.S. Marshal stating that he located and arrested the individual that we had been looking for. This U.S. Marshal stated that they had found him working as a janitor at a school in Ft. Lauderdale. I found this a bit odd, the fact that this guy had a job and was in Ft. Lauderdale, but it wasn't entirely out of the question. Anyway, I jumped in my OGV and drove to the federal courthouse in Ft. Lauderdale. While I was driving there, I received another phone call from the same U.S. Marshal. He proceeded to tell me that something was definitely wrong. He went on to say that the guy in custody swore that it wasn't him and that we had the wrong guy. I remember responding, "Yeah, but they all say that." The U.S. Marshal responded that he agreed but this time it was different. The guy was actually believable. So, I told him that I would be there in about 30 minutes and that we would sort it out then.

I got to the courthouse just when the initial appearance was about the get started. That's when I first laid eyes on the individual in custody. Let me tell you, my heart dropped! It definitely wasn't him. I mean, it wasn't even close. I had seen a photo of the individual we were looking for the day of the proffer, and this guy wasn't even close. So, I grabbed the U.S. Marshal and told him that we needed to speak outside quickly. He followed me outside into the hallway, and I told him that it was the wrong guy! After I told him the whole story, we both decided very quickly and unanimously that we had no choice but to go back into the court room and tell the judge the truth and exactly what happened.

We did so, after which the charges were immediately dropped, and the individual was released. We then asked the individual if we could talk to him quickly so we could explain. He was fuming and **really** pissed off but agreed. Of course, we first apologized profusely, over and over. Then we explained exactly what we did during the investigation that led to his arrest. When we mentioned the driver's license, the individual's face lit up. He stated that his driver's license had been stolen recently, and it had to be this guy that we had encountered in the parking lot. When we asked who this person was, he said that it was one of his wife's relatives, a cousin he believed. And this guy, he referred to him as Pierre, must have stolen his driver's license and then used it as identification when the surveillance officers stopped him that day after they observed him conducting counter surveillance. Man, was I hot!

You see, this suspect that we had just released and the individual actually on scene that day, this Pierre character, didn't look anything alike. Not even close! And those officers on scene that day never picked up on that. I mean, this guy that we had just released weighed a good 250 pounds. The one conducting counter surveillance was about 120 pounds. And not one officer on scene that day thought it odd that their target had dropped about 130 pounds? You have to remember that I wasn't there the day of the arrest. I wasn't there the day of the proffer. I couldn't make my own observations or ask my own questions. I could only rely on what they told me happened and what I could glean from reading their reports. Anyway, we had a more pressing issue.

The individual we had was really angry and frustrated as he should have been. We fucked up. Period. And he was also deeply embarrassed. He was a janitor at a local school and had been arrested inside the school in front of teachers, staff and students. The U.S. Marshal and I decided that we had to do our best for this guy and go to his school. We proceeded to do so and met with the principal. We explained the entire story and did the best we could to make it right for the guy. Thank God the principal understood and said that the individual was a very good worker and that he wouldn't be fired. That was good, but there wasn't much else we could do. What happened had happened. We couldn't go back and change it.

To make matters worse, a few weeks later I received a phone call from Chief Counsel's Office at DEA Headquarters. They regretfully had to inform me that I was getting sued by that same individual for false arrest and imprisonment. Great, just great. The guy who had the least culpability in the whole matter was the one getting sued. And I wasn't even there that day! Talk about no good deed going unpunished. When I asked the lady on the phone why me, she was super nice. She took the time to explain that it was because I worked for the big, bad government. The other officers involved worked for a local police department. She said that the individual we had arrested must have been told by friends or family or just decided on his own to talk to an attorney. And as soon as the attorney heard the words federal government or DEA, he must have seen dollar signs and told the person to sue us. Well, sue me.

Getting back to the conversation, I was really nervous that I was going to lose my job. I mean, I was getting **sued**. However, the lady on the phone was really nice and politely explained that as long as I was acting in the scope of my duty, which I was, nothing would happen to me. I was still nervous. She then gave me a laundry list of the stuff she needed – mostly reports of investigation – but also witness statements from all who were present the day of the arrest, as well as one from me. I got off the phone dejected with a mountain of paperwork to take care of when a senior agent who sat next to me at the time and had overheard the conversation stated something I will never forget. He said, "Kid, if you don't get sued at least once in your career, you aren't doing your job right." That made me feel a little better...a little.

A few weeks went by while I slowly completed everything asked of me by Chief Counsels Office. Gradually, I was able to get back into the swing of things and get back into my investigations. Actually, I kind of forgot about the whole issue. Then one day a few weeks later, I received a phone call from the same lady who proceeded to tell me that I had been cleared of any wrongdoing. Whew! What a relief! I couldn't help but ask what was going to happen next. She calmly told me that nothing was going to happen and that the matter had been closed. I was so confused. And when I tried to ask for more details, she curtly cut me off and said that the matter had been closed and that they had settled out of court with the individual. She then stated that she really couldn't say anything else due to certain agreements each party had decided such as, I'm sure, how much he was awarded!

That stayed with me a very long time, and I still think about it to this day. I did nothing wrong and got sued. Then instead of fighting for me, the DEA or the U.S. Department of Justice or whoever, just paid him off? Without fighting? I remember discussing it with that same senior agent. He replied that it happened all the time and that the government figured that it was easier to throw $10,000 or $20,000 or whatever at the situation instead of all the work it would take to fight it and investigate it. He stated that the manpower and the time spent on the investigation, possibly travel to interview witnesses, etc., would have probably cost even more than the settlement. So, when the money was added on top of the fact that they were looking at a six-month investigation or longer, the government just saw it as not only less of a hassle but cheaper too. I don't know. I guess so but it never sat well with me.

Guy Lewis (left) and myself enjoy a cocktail at the DEA Christmas party.

KEITH LEIGHTON

17
The Mendez Brothers

"Loose Lips Sink Ships"
— U.S. War Advertising Council

Between the time that I had first attended the Noriega sentencing and this moment to date in Group 9, a number of other agents in my group were working on a separate long-term investigation in which I became involved. During the investigation of Noriega, agents and prosecutors had learned that four Colombian brothers — John Mendez, James Mendez, Lewis Mendez, and Saul Mendez — were close associates of Pablo Escobar and members the Medellin Cartel and that these brothers were living in the South Florida area. Because of this, a decision was made to investigate them.

The problem was that we had no way of infiltrating these brothers. With some help from our Intelligence Analysts and good old-fashioned surveillance work, we were able to locate the four brothers and identify their residences. But this was a small part of any investigation. We can follow people around all day, but it doesn't always lead to any kind of criminal activity, especially when we are at the level of these brothers. Members of a drug trafficking organization who are at that level as far as the hierarchy goes or the chain of command, let all of the plebes and rubes underneath them do all of the dirty work and "hands on" jobs. We spent days and days on end following them around, but all they did was errands, chores, go out to eat, go to the gym, etc. In a nutshell, surveillance was just one of many, many investigative techniques and was usually only successful when used in conjunction with a variety of other investigative techniques. The bottom line was that surveillance rarely worked on its own. We needed more.

What was frustrating to us was that we didn't have any other investigative measures to use. We didn't have an informant into the group. Even if we had an available informant, high-level organizations such as this one really only trusted relatives and associates that they have known their entire lives. Without a viable informant, we couldn't introduce an undercover because the informant would be needed to make the introduction. We considered a wiretap but after a brief preliminary investigation into the cell phones that they were using, we determined that they each carried three to four cell phones at a time and they traded all of them in almost weekly. Thus, a wiretap investigation was out. We did manage to put up a hidden camera on Lewis's house, but it didn't reveal much. We went down the list of techniques trying to find a way to infiltrate the brothers, but all we could come up with was one...and it was risky. But we had no choice by this time...

We decided to do a grand jury investigation, a grand jury investigation using the people who would know the Mendez brothers the best − prisoners serving time. We would find defendants who were presently incarcerated that either had knowledge of the Mendez drug trafficking organization or knew of someone else who did. We would then interview them and whoever else dealt with the Mendez brothers and then put them before a sitting grand jury once a week for testimony. Guy Lewis would do the questioning. We did this week after week after week. And if the prisoner was out of the area or out of state, we had the U.S. Marshals transport them to a local jail in South Florida (the U.S. Marshals are responsible for this task too in the federal system − transporting federal prisoners. Remember the movie "Con Air?" Same thing). The plan was to build up to a sizeable amount of information and then indict all four brothers on conspiracy. This grand jury investigation went on for about a year, but during the entire time, we were wary of one thing.

And we were right on the money, unfortunately.

The first problem with an investigation like this was that prisoners were almost always bored. And as much as we told each and every one of them to not tell anyone what was happening with our investigation or what took place in the grand jury, when we interviewed as many prisoners as we did during that investigation, one of them was bound to talk. They talked to their bunkmates, and to their spouses and to their moms. They talked to someone. All they had was time. They spent a lot of that time talking. We knew it, but this was the only shot we had. The other problem was logistics. As I said earlier, a lot of these prisoners had to be moved around and transported into South Florida from other parts of the country. Of course, when these prisoners returned, they were met with all kinds of questions from other inmates. Questions like where they had been or where they went or why they were gone so long. All gave the impression that the defendant was cooperating with law enforcement, or "snitching" which was the worst offense in prison. So, many of our prisoner witnesses backed out for fear of retaliation or harm to themselves or harm to their families on the outside. It was just a toxic situation. Unfortunately, the word was bound to get out. And it did!

Within a matter of months, all four brothers left the Miami area and fled back to Colombia. Down the road we learned that they had indeed been tipped off about the pending indictment. Nevertheless, we did indict them. They were indicted for conspiracy to possess with the intent to distribute hundreds of thousands of kilograms of cocaine (yes, you read that right.) over a ten-year period. At the time, it was the largest cocaine indictment in the state of Florida. Eerily enough, but not surprising in the drug game, once the power had shifted from the Medellin Cartel to the Cali Cartel, three of the four brothers were never heard from again. No one knew what happened to them. The only one that resurfaced was Saul Mendez. He was detained by Panamanian authorities as he attempted to travel to Mexico and was sent to Miami where he was arrested.

A press release from the DEA Miami Field Division and the U.S. Attorney's Office in the Southern District of Florida (SDFL), stated that he pled guilty to one count of conspiracy to possess with intent to distribute more than five kilograms of cocaine, in violation of Title 21, United States Code, Sections 846 and 841(a)(1). It went on to state that Mendez, along with his brothers Lewis Mendez, James Mendez and John Mendez, were indicted in 1994 pursuant to their roles as drug trafficking for Pablo Escobar and the Medellin cartel. On March 18, 2011, Saul Mendez was detained by Panamanian authorities while attempting to travel to Mexico, and then flown to Miami, Florida, where he was arrested by the DEA.

The release went on to say that between 1979 and 1994, Saul Mendez and his brothers – Lewis, James and John – under the direction of Escobar, were sent to Miami to run Escobar's drug trafficking operations. They proceeded to distribute thousand-kilogram loads of cocaine throughout the United States.

Court documents obtained in support of this indictment were able to show that the Mendez brothers owned multiple properties and businesses in the Miami area on behalf of Escobar. These properties and businesses were used to facilitate the drug trafficking activities of Saul Mendez and his brothers. Additionally, these properties and businesses were used to conceal shipments of U.S. currency from Florida back to Colombia. On one occasion, in November of 1989, Saul Mendez ordered a money courier to travel from New York City to Miami with approximately $3,000,000 concealed in boxes. This same U.S. currency was then transported to Escobar and the Medellin Cartel.

Information was also obtained during this investigation which indicated that Saul and his brothers were enforcers for Escobar. On one occasion in December of 1988, the Mendez brothers sent an individual back to Colombia to meet with Escobar. The issue? This individual was in charge of guarding a stash house and managed to lose over 500 kilograms of cocaine to a rival drug trafficking organization. This individual was told to personally explain the loss to Escobar.[1] (*Please refer to a Reference appendix for a link to the original press releases and articles summarized in my story.*)

18
Operation Zorro II/Administrators Award

bout this time in my career, I had earned the reputation of being a pretty solid agent. I had done a number of buy-bust operations, testified in federal and state court a number of times, travelled quite a bit, made numerous arrests and seized a lot of money. But I wanted more. Almost all of my investigations up to that point were in Miami, all what we refer to as local impact investigations. Now, don't get me wrong. These were very critical investigations and crucial to our mission, but the DEA was the number one drug enforcement agency in the world. We only had one responsibility – to investigate violations of the U.S. Controlled Substance Act which was United States Code (U.S.C.) Title 21. That was it. We were the only single mission agency in the world. Compare that to an agency like the FBI who was responsible for 108 different crimes. All we enforced was one. I might have been biased, but we were the best at what we did. Because it was all that we did. I'll be honest, I wanted to be James Bond! I wanted that international flair. I wanted a bigger stage. And I soon got it.

One day a new Assistant Special Agent in Charge had arrived. Basically, the way the hierarchy went in a large DEA office was that we had the SAC, then one or two Associate Special Agents in Charge (A/SACs), depending on the size of the office, four ASACs and about 12 Group Supervisors (G/Ss). Again, the exact number depended on the size of the office. This new ASAC had been very involved in wiretap investigations during his career in the New York office. And he wanted to see Group 9 in the Miami office become more involved in these types of investigations. He wanted us to go beyond arresting Johnny Greensneakers selling crack on the street corner. He wanted us to find out where Mr. Greensneakers got his crack from, and then where that person got his crack from and where.... well, you get the idea. He wanted us to get to the source of supply, even if we traced it back to Colombia. He wanted us to work hand in hand with headquarters in an effort to find the command-and-control telephone number of the organization, basically the hierarchy.

Back in those days, the only part of the Miami office that was working wiretap investigations were our two HIDTA groups. HIDTA stands for High Intensity Drug Trafficking Area. Agents assigned to those groups were the big boys at the time. If you were lucky enough to get assigned to one of those groups, you chased around guys like Pablo Escobar, Carlos Lehder and members of the Medellin Cartel. They were specialized groups. But what my ASAC was trying to say at the time was that these groups didn't own the market on wiretap investigations. He was saying that any group could work them since high-level complex drug trafficking organizations, what we call DTOs, are a dime a dozen in Miami. And he wanted his groups to start working them. It was music to my ears.

After some politicking with the SAC at the time, this new ASAC was able to convince the agents assigned to the HIDTA groups to put on a one-day seminar for the rest of the offices about these investigations. He wanted the agenda to include how to find a command-and-control number, how to write the wiretap affidavit, how to run the operational side of the investigation – the staffing of the wire room, the scheduling of surveillance teams, the whole gamut. I attended this seminar and thought it was utterly fascinating. This was **exactly** why I had joined the DEA. If we were able to write this affidavit and convince a federal judge that this telephone number was being used to control a DTO, we would be able to listen to their conversations. We would have a front row seat to their entire operation. It would be laid out right in front of us and all we had to do was listen. Before I go on, I know that I made that sound incredibly easy. But it's not. First, we had to first find the telephone number that we were going to tap, and that wasn't always the easiest task. Let's say that an informant knew someone who sold a lot of drugs but didn't know his phone number. However, he did know a few phone numbers utilized by a couple of his DTO members and also this guy's girlfriend. We would then have to take these three numbers and submit an Administrative Subpoena for these numbers asking for all numbers that **each** number called from their phone for the past 30 or 60 days. And then we'd have to research, analyze and sort all of these numbers by hand (computers and the internet were still not in use) to try to find that **one** common number among the three. The result was usually a pretty good bet that it was our guy.

Then came the affidavit. Understand that the only way a federal judge was going to authorize us to intercept telephone communications was to convince him or her of a couple of key points. The first was that the organization we were targeting better be in the upper echelon of the drug trafficking world in our area. They had better be the best of the best. These were organizations that had hierarchy, that had a solid structure and that could import multi-hundred-kilogram cocaine loads into the U.S. Second, we had to convince the same federal judge that you have attempted **everything** you could as far as investigative tools to infiltrate this DTO and have either failed or the method simply wasn't possible. We needed to convince him or her that this wiretap affidavit was the **only** way to infiltrate this DTO and was basically a last resort. In a nutshell, we needed to explain why or how the following investigative tools and techniques have either failed, were unavailable, or simply weren't an option.

These tools included surveillance, undercover agents, informants, grand jury testimony, etc. But it could be done if you had the right agent and that agent was me. I was so ready, and I couldn't wait to get started.

After a couple of misfires, I finally got my chance. Actually, the chance developed from one of these misfires. The Los Angeles office was up on a wiretap and they started intercepting a member of the DTO who was in New York. So, they passed the telephone number and the content of the conversations to the New York office who proceeded to write their affidavit and initiate their wiretap investigation on that DTO member's cell phone. Almost immediately, that same number in New York started calling yet another member of the DTO, this one residing and operating in Miami. Once again, the cell phone number and contents of the calls were forwarded down to... you guessed it, my group – Group 9.

However, I was kind of screwed over when the lead was passed to another agent in my group who had less time on the job than I, but these things happened. No biggie. I just kept my head down and kept working. My time would come. I just had to be patient and bide my time. However, it was a good waiting period during which I used to my advantage. I watched the investigation develop. I watched how the affidavit was carefully constructed. To say an affidavit was written wouldn't give it due credit. It was a major, major project, one that was more like a construction project pieced together and built over time until completed, which was why I used the word constructed and not written. I mean, when completed, an average wiretap affidavit was approximately 90 pages! That's the size of some novels!!

So, I waited and I learned. One interesting thing I learned, which took a while to get used to, was the fact that the target, the actual target of a wiretap affidavit, was not a member of the DTO or even a person at all but the actual phone. This took a while to get used to because it was the phone that was the instrument on which the incriminating calls were placed. Of course, the object was to make the arrest of the person using the phone, but as far as the affidavit went the target was the phone. It actually made it easier for us because that meant that we could complete the affidavit without knowing who was actually holding, carrying, or using the cell phone.

After waiting for so long, approximately six months after the first line went up, I finally had my chance. Another drug dealer in Miami surfaced and was speaking to the main target of the first line on a regular basis. It was what we referred to as a spin-off. I jumped at the chance and immediately starting writing while also researching everything I would need – telephone subscriber reports (basically who owns the phone), telephone toll records (toll calls), call detail records (incoming and outgoing calls) – all obtained by the issuance of administrative subpoenas.

As the information came in from the various cell phone companies, I did the best that I could to organize and analyze it, but it was just too much. I needed help. Every DEA office had intelligence analysts who assisted the agents with their investigations, but back then only one or two responsible to the whole division existed, which was just not enough. Thankfully the Miami office had just hired a new Intelligence Analyst right out of college. I met her on her first day in the office and, although I felt bad in doing this, I jumped at the chance and solicited her assistance before she could even move into her desk. Believe me, if I had waited, it would have been a feeding frenzy since intelligence analysts were so in demand at the time. I had my intelligence analyst. Next, I needed a prosecutor.

I lucked out on this as well. Just like intelligence analysts, federal prosecutors in Miami back then were very much in demand, at least the good ones. It just so happened that the federal prosecutor handling the first wiretap investigation had a new federal prosecutor fresh from the State Attorney's Office under his wing. She was on probation and reporting to the prosecutor, so he recommended her to work with me. The two wiretap investigations were tied together, and now the two federal prosecutors were, too. It was all under the same roof, so to speak, and beginning to come together.

The next tool I needed was a device that was activated as soon as the caller made or received a call. Basically, when that happened, the outgoing or incoming call is routed right to a device that sat in our office. And we'd get the outgoing or incoming number at the exact same time the call was made. It was a huge benefit since all of the aforementioned toll record information and call detail information was good to have, but it's all past information. Those records weren't real time. This device gave us the exact same information but in real time. It made a huge difference. It did require probable cause and a court order signed by a judge, and it didn't allow us to hear the conversations, but it was a great investigative tool to have. That much was done.

After months of meetings with the prosecutor, analyzing hundreds of pages of telephone records, and constantly working on an affidavit, it was finally done and ready to be signed by a federal judge. This was November, 1995. I worked every day during this time period. There was so much to be done. I oversaw the wire room operation which entailed scheduling contracted Spanish speaking monitors who listened to all the phone calls every day from 8:00 a.m. to midnight. I also was in charge of both the wire room schedule and the surveillance schedule.

The wire room needed to be manned by an agent, and we needed agents on the streets who could move at a moment's notice to cover a drug meeting or drug deal or money pick-up that had just been heard and discussed over the telephone line that we were listening to. And then there were meetings with the prosecutor about how everything was developing, meetings with my superiors about the same, and keeping up with the mountains of paperwork that the U.S. Government was notorious for. Additionally, I had to keep the judge up to speed. When we did a wiretap investigation, the judge required what is referred to as a 10-day report. After 10 days of interceptions, I had to put together a document that contained a synopsis of the investigation to date along with a sample of a few phone calls so that he or she could see that we were making progress. Although the wiretap was judicially authorized, a federal judge needed to be sure we were listening for the right reasons, that the sworn affidavit supporting the wiretap was truthful and legitimate, and that the calls we were intercepting were incriminating calls, or what we referred to as "dirty" calls.

Slowly during the rest of 1995 and into 1996, we started identifying all of the members of the organization. We started with one phone and eventually went on to receive approval for tapping five other phones associated with members of this organization. Not at the same time, mind you, but the whole idea of a true, successful wiretap investigation is to move up the chain and to advance up the hierarchy of the organization. And that's exactly what we did, all the way to the number one guy in Colombia. I was so proud of myself. I had done it. I was running a wiretap investigation with the DEA that went all the way to the source in Colombia.

I'd like to explain one of the other incredible benefits of a wiretap investigation, and a fact that I would harp on and stress in my later years as a Title III wiretap investigation instructor with headquarters. Making arrests and seizures in our investigation was all well and good. After all, it was what we did. It was our mission and it was what we got paid to do. But there was more – paying it forward. Very rarely was a wiretap initiated without a lead or a "dirty call" that came from another office. That's exactly what happened with that first wiretap in my office – we received a "dirty call" from the New York office. Then that first wiretap in my office spun me up on the wiretap that I was presently working. And we needed to do the same, not only to pass investigative leads to our fellow DEA agents so that they can make great cases but also to infiltrate, investigate, dismantle, and destroy the entire organization throughout the entire United States from top to bottom, from the target in large cities like Miami, New York, and Los Angeles who were importing multi-hundred-kilogram loads of cocaine, all the way down to rural areas of the country where crack cocaine from the same loads of cocaine, were being sold on the street corners – and every middleman, broker, mid-level dealer, transporter, courier, financier, money launderer, and stash house operator in between. I'll explain more in a bit.

We gradually started to pick-off some great phone calls which led to a couple of fantastic seizures. On March 8, 1996, we received a phone call about counting money in a stash house in Miami. We immediately contacted our surveillance units out on the street via radio and asked them to respond to the area where we believed the stash house was located. Normally, the phone calls were very cryptic and often in code, so a lot of the times we were in the dark as far as identities of people and locations were concerned.

But this time we got lucky. The incoming caller this time identified himself and stated that he was on the way with the money now. To our amazement, and actually amusement, he asked our main target if the address of 254 N. Main Street (fictitious) was the right address. Of course, our target was irate and told him to NEVER say that on the phone and then, after a few expletives in Spanish, proceeded to hang up on the caller immediately. But it was too late. We had the address.

Within minutes we had surveillance units on the house. A little while later we watched a vehicle pull up and then observed the driver walk into the house with a large duffel bag slung over his shoulder. We knew we had hit a home run. A few minutes after he left, we did in DEA what's referred to as an approach. It was basically an encounter with the occupant of the house. It took place when we believed that there was illegal activity going on inside the house, but we didn't have enough time to obtain a search warrant. We usually got consent to search only because if we didn't, we'd just secure the location and head to the office to attempt to complete a search warrant with whatever probable cause we had.

Anyway, we had a couple of agents knock on the door to try to engage the individual inside to get a feel for his nervousness, appearance, etc., basically anything that we could use in a search warrant. The two agents proceeded to do that and noticed that the resident of the house was very nervous. They told the resident that they had received information from a reliable source that the house was involved in drug trafficking and would he mind answering a few questions. The resident was sweating profusely and was visibly upset. At this point, the two agents used their training well and asked if they could look around since the resident seemed really nervous about something.

They then proceeded to ask for consent to search the residence, and they got it. The resident agreed to let them in. And low and behold the agents eventually made their way to one of the upstairs bedrooms where they found $344,450 in U.S. Currency on the floor of the bedroom that was being collected to be sent back to Colombia. **Pay dirt!!**

$344,450.00 U.S. Currency seized during the "Operation Zorro II" investigation

We asked the resident if the money was his to which he immediately denied any responsibility, saying that he didn't live there and was just visiting and that he didn't even know the money was there. We knew that was total bullshit as he had been intercepted numerous times on the wiretap as the stash house operator who was responsible for collecting drug proceeds destined for Colombia for the organization. So, we proceeded to seize the money. Since having cash wasn't illegal, we didn't have to arrest the individual. That was perfect for our investigation because if we had to arrest him, the discovery process would have started almost immediately. The discovery process is the process of turning all of your evidence over to the defense counsel prior to trial for examination and so that they can prepare a defense. It was a win-win.

Even though it seemed as if he had gotten off scot-free that day even when he was a member of the organization, he didn't. We just simply waited until the end of the entire operation and then proceeded to obtain Grand Jury indictments on every member of the organization, including that individual. One morning, we decided to round everyone up and ended up arresting 20 or 30 or more people all in the same day.

It started to become quite difficult to keep the wiretap going while making sure drugs weren't sold and distributed right under our noses while we just sat back and watched. We had to get very creative when it came to situations like that. We did whatever we could but it wasn't easy.

We were able to make another pretty impressive seizure, one I would never forget. It's important to keep in mind that these organizations were run like businesses. Everything was basically the same as a legit business except for the commodity – cocaine. They were meticulous, precise, extremely intelligent, and ruthless. They would do anything to sell their product. It was **all** about the Benjamins to them. And they knew that we were always around and always watching. We were in the cities, on the highways, in bus stations and in airports. This particular seizure came one day after intercepting a phone call about a female flying out of Miami International Airport with a large amount of currency with her and destined for Colombia. We didn't have a name or a description as they used some kind of street name when referring to her. All we knew was that it was a female.

We sent a few agents out to the airport to watch the flight and to see if we could locate her. It sounded simple, but you had to remember that this was Miami and a flight to Bogota, Colombia, no matter what time of day or night or time of year, was **always** packed. So, we needed to find this female in a crowd of 200 plus passengers. Not an easy task! I've always been a big believer of the old adage that it was better to be lucky than good and that was so true in this case.

One of the agents with us that day in the airport decided to chat with one of the ticket agents to see if she had noticed anything strange about any of the passengers while checking them in. These airline employees were like gold mines of information, and we used them all the time. They saw passengers every day and could tell when something was odd, slightly off, or just not right.

At first, she said no but then kind of made an off the cuff remark about this one female passenger who took this flight every couple of weeks but used a Dutch passport. She added that she always thought it was strange since this person lived in Miami and traveled back and forth to Colombia, a place not populated by a whole lot of Dutch citizens. That kind of piqued our interest as we also thought it was kind of odd. Since we had struck out finding this female otherwise, we figured we would find this person and interview her. What could it hurt?

With the help of the same airline employee, we found her and started asking her a few questions. At first, all of us were in serious doubt that this was the person we were looking for. She was petite, about five feet tall, and weighed about 100 pounds. Plus, she was dressed really nicely in designer clothes. This clearly was not who we were looking for. However, one of the guys insisted that we talk to her. As I was thinking that this was going to be a waste of time, all of a sudden, she started getting really confused. She couldn't remember some simple answers to questions that we always asked people who we suspected of carrying drugs or money. How long were you going for? Business or pleasure? Who were you staying with in Bogota? How did you get here to the airport? Simple stuff like that. But she couldn't answer any of them. What a lucky break! So, we quickly contacted U.S. Customs and requested that one of their female officers take the female back into secondary – basically, a private room for interviewing and further screening.

This was eventually done and the results were shocking. This female turned out to be the principal money courier for the organization. They utilized her because they thought she looked so

not like a drug dealer or money courier. As I said previously, she was thin, small, attractive, and wore nice clothes, and the Dutch passport was used to throw law enforcement off. When she was screened, she was found to have $300,000 in U.S. currency on her person. Stacks of hundred-dollar bills were layered all around her legs. She had money in fake pockets that had been sewn into her jacket.

The time was still pre-9-1-1, and TSA was years from being implemented, so there was no high-tech screening like there is now. Back then all you did was go through a metal detector. Anyway, I was flabbergasted!! The money was seized but she was also released until that day of reckoning came down the road as I explained earlier. She was eventually arrested later during our take down.

$300,000.00 U.S. Currency seized from the female courier at Miami International Airport during the "Operation Zorro II" investigation.

As I mentioned above, it was paramount to get other offices spun up on phone lines from the leads, tips and "dirty calls" we forwarded on to them. By this point of the investigation, the first wiretap that started in my office spun up the Newark, NJ office. Eventually, the Newark office spun up the Chicago, IL office. The wiretap for which I was the case agent, had spun up the Houston, TX office. And it went on. It was an amazing thing to be part of. By the time this investigation had been completed, approximately a year and a half after it had started, 16 different offices had initiated a wiretap investigation at some point of that year connected with the **same exact** organization.

When it was completed, 167 individuals had been arrested nationwide and 5,600 kilograms of cocaine had been seized along with $13 million in assets. It had never been done before. And, honestly, I don't think it has been done since. It was an unprecedented task. And it paid great benefits to the agents who tirelessly worked it. Personally, I received a hand-written letter from the U.S. Attorney General at the time, Janet Reno. I was also the recipient of the Administrators Award which was the highest award given out in DEA. Additionally, I was promoted to a Senior Special Agent which came with a pretty hefty pay raise.

Proud recipients of the DEA Administrator's Award for the work we did in the "Operation Zorro II" investigation. DEA Administrator Thomas Constantine is in the middle. I am second from the right.

This investigation had lasted approximately a year and a half from beginning to end. All in all, I was the affiant on 23 separate wiretap affidavits. That included the original five targets of the investigation plus numerous continuations or extension affidavits since each affidavit was only valid for a 30-day time period. By this time, I had become an expert on writing these affidavits.

Because of my experience, I was asked by headquarters to join their Cellular Telephone Exploitation Team and travel throughout the United States teaching Title III Wiretap Techniques and Methods to other agents and TFOs. It was a pretty neat gig. It got me out of the office once in a while and gave me the opportunity to travel a bit which was a nice way to break things up. About once a month, I packed a suitcase and traveled with the team to a different part of the country to teach these classes. I remember teaching in Dallas, Houston, Ft. Lauderdale, Atlanta, and Philadelphia. That was enjoyable while it lasted. But it didn't last long.

Office of the Attorney General
Washington, B. C. 20530

Mr. Keith P. Leighton
Special Agent
Drug Enforcement Administration
Miami Division
8400 N.W. 53rd Street
Miami, FL 33166

Dear Mr. Leighton:

I would like to take this opportunity to compliment you for your excellent work in the Zorro II investigation.

This investigation was unprecedented in scope, targeting first the drug suppliers of the Cali Cartel and then the so-called Mexican Federation, the organization responsible for transporting the Cartel drugs across the US-Mexico border. Takedown of both sides of this illicit operation would not have been possible without your dedication and perseverance in the investigation.

In addition, the unprecedented coordination and cooperation of all the federal, state and local agencies involved in Zorro II deserves a special commendation. Each of you were required to coordinate your efforts with the investigations proceeding in the other districts, from the numerous applications for electronic surveillance to the timing of the final arrests on the last takedown day in May of 1996. Thanks to your teamwork and professionalism, each district realized its full potential, bringing the investigation to an impressive conclusion.

I extend the Department's appreciation for your efforts to date and for the continued hard work and cooperation that I know will follow during the prosecution of these cases.

Sincerely,

Janet Reno

cc: Thomas A. Constantine
      DEA Administrator

Personal, handwritten letter on parchment paper, dated Nov 1, 1996, and personally signed by Janet Reno, Attorney General at the time congratulating me on the Operation Zorro II investigation.

19
Jaime

One of the pitfalls of the drug trade was the violence associated with it. It always depressed me. And now I might have witnessed it. I'm not sure. After we made all of the arrests when the wiretap investigation had been concluded, one of the individuals we arrested was a Colombian national. I'll just refer to him by his first name, Jaime.

After his arrest, Jaime cooperated immediately. He came to the table and told us **everything** he knew about the organization. He was honest, forthright, and intelligent. He was very well mannered, very well spoken, and had a great sense of humor. He wasn't the typical drug dealer at all. He looked like the typical businessman which wasn't that far from the truth since he handled the financial affairs of the organization.

Jaime was eventually sentenced and went off to jail. Eventually, I went my own way, as well, to an overseas position. While I was overseas, I kept in close contact with my old buddies back in Group 9. I remember hearing from them that Jaime wanted to cooperate with the DEA after he was released from prison. They said that he felt guilty for what he had done, and even after doing his time, he wanted to help fight the drug trade. I thought that was admirable, so I kept up with the situation the best that I could.

Years later, I learned that Jaime had eventually been released from prison after serving his sentence. Just as the law demands, since Jaime wasn't a U.S. citizen, he was deported back to Colombia immediately after his release from prison. All convicted felons were deported if they weren't U.S. citizens. I guess he asked some of the agents who were still assigned to Group 9 what he should do. They told him that if he really wanted to work for the DEA, then he should go to the DEA office in Bogota. Jaime told them that he was going to do this as soon as he got settled. The Bogota office was given a heads up that this individual might stop in one day. That never happened. He never went to the DEA office in Bogota. And no one ever heard from Jaime again.

You just never know. Maybe he got cold feet. Maybe he changed his mind. I hope so. I don't know. It just didn't seem like him. He always kept in touch with us. I mean, he called me in Brussels! He called me collect from jail, but still! I always feared the worst, especially if word got out that Jaime cooperated with us and told us everything about the operation. That wouldn't have been good. That wouldn't have been good at all

20
Honey Bare

Just a quick funny side story. While working these long wiretap investigations mentioned earlier, I became pretty close with the agents in New York, Los Angeles, and Houston. Throughout the year and a half investigation, we were constantly in touch with one another, passing leads and coordinating activities since, after all, we were all investigating the same organization, just different parts of it. And these contacts assisted me in a very strange encounter down the road.

Soon after the wiretap investigation had concluded, I received a call from the Los Angeles office. During this call, I was asked to assist with one of their on-going wiretap investigations. The agent on the phone explained that they had picked up a conversation in which the organization they were investigating talked about using a stripper from Las Vegas to travel to Miami to pick up 18 kilograms of cocaine and then return to Los Angeles.

The agent stated that at first, they had no idea where she was going to receive the cocaine or where she was staying, and that was why they hadn't contacted us until that day. The agent then explained that they had just received a call from this female stripper informing the main target in Los Angeles that she had made it, had picked up the cocaine, and was leaving from the Shangri La Motel (fictitious) in the morning. She had slipped and given up her location. The agent wanted to know if there was any way we could roll out on surveillance on that motel and watch her as she left and then attempt to stop her. The agent stated that it would be a great way for us to make an arrest and seizure and also allow them to continue their investigation without compromising the wiretap since the arrest and seizure would be made approximately 3,000 miles away in Miami. I responded that we would love to help them and that we knew exactly where that motel was located. So, we immediately hit the street and established surveillance on the motel.

It was almost too easy, and I actually felt bad for a second.... just for a second. After all, she was a drug dealer just like the rest of them, just not a very smart one. When we established surveillance on the motel that afternoon, we observed an old, beat up SUV with Nevada plates in the parking lot. This was almost too easy, almost like shooting fish in a barrel.

Honey Bare!

After about two hours of sitting and waiting, we observed a female approach the vehicle and get in. We couldn't see what room she came out of, but she had left the motel office, so we were pretty sure that she had checked out. We observed the SUV depart and proceeded to initiate a mobile surveillance on the SUV. We eventually made a traffic stop based on probable cause which resulted in the seizure of 18 kilograms of cocaine located in a suitcase in the rear hatchback area of the SUV.

The amusing part of this story is that during the booking/processing of the female, she admitted that she was a stripper in Las Vegas. She stated that her stage name was Honey Bare. She said that she danced at the Palomino Club in Las Vegas and that I should come and check out her show at some point. She then handed me a promotional flyer containing numerous nude photos of her in all kinds of different outfits. I still have that portfolio, by the way. Unfortunately, I had to break it to Honey Bare that my visit would have to wait for about five to 10 years because she was going to a whole new club. This one was called Club Fed, as in, jail.

21
Brussels, Belgium

ver since I was a kid, I was fascinated by James Bond. I had always wanted to be an international spy racing all around the world saving mankind from the likes of Dr. No, SPECTRE, and Blofield. I loved international travel and was lucky enough to have been able to travel to both Cologne, Germany and London, England for case work while I was assigned to the Miami office. Back to Bond. I loved how smooth and suave he was. I loved the cars and the gadgets. Yes, I knew that it was all fictional and totally unrealistic, but I wanted to be as close as I could to that.

As stated previously, DEA had a huge international footprint. Around 1997, I began submitting my name for assignments throughout Europe as they surfaced. I was so fascinated with the idea of James Bond and my two European work trips that I really wanted to go to someplace in Europe as opposed to South or Central America. I was following a dream. The way it worked with DEA at that time was that a posting would be released asking for interest in a certain foreign assignment, a solicitation for interest. Interested agents would then submit their names and eventually after gathering all of the names, headquarters would then decide. This sounded pretty straightforward, but I soon learned that this involved a **ton** of politics and "who you know" mentality. At that time, I was pretty well known throughout the Miami office and some elements of headquarters as I had done a few high-level investigations by that time in my career. But I was soon to find out that this was just the tip of the iceberg.

The first job that was posted was Rome. I couldn't believe my luck (as if I had a chance in hell of landing Rome in my very first attempt!). So, I immediately submitted my name. It was for a three-year tour and required either knowledge of the Italian language or a six-month stint at language school in Washington, D.C., which was sponsored by the U.S. State Department since U.S. Embassies and Consulates fell under their area of responsibility, among many other duties. I soon found out that the majority of foreign offices were physically located in the host country's U.S. Embassy or Consulate.

I was then asked to provide some additional information, such as my previous assignments, past evaluations, etc., kind of like a bio sheet. After that, I was informed that the next step would be the completion of a Best Qualified list or commonly referred to in DEA circles as the BQ list. This was a list of names chosen jointly by both the headquarters foreign operations section and the Country Attaché of the host country, which was really just a fancy name for a group supervisor. Obviously, he or she would have a huge say in who was picked for the job since that person would be working directly for him or her. The Country Attaché had a vested interest in who was chosen which only makes sense. I eventually made the BQ list and was on top of the world. Italy, here I come. Ciao!! But I had no idea about the real process, the behind-the-scenes process.

Little did I know at that point that when it came to the primo spots around the world, in this case Europe, it was normal for over 100 agents to submit their names for a posting like Rome. And many of the agents on the list were rock stars who had dismantled major drug trafficking organizations and cartels almost by themselves. I was in serious company. I soon learned that after headquarters and the Country Attaché had read and reviewed all of the names, applications and bio sheets, they would then actually form a list of who they wanted the most. An actual ranking list. And of course, this info was always being leaked. I was constantly hearing, "Hey, I heard from a buddy who knows someone who knows someone who knows the Country Attaché that you're number one on the list!!" Stuff like that. And then the following week I was told that I had slipped to the top five or something like that. It drove me bat-shit crazy! How did I drop from number one to the top five in a week when I hadn't done anything? It was a moving target, and yet my life in Miami, 3,000 miles away, was the exact same.

It was only when a senior agent noticed my frustration, did I finally understand the politics involved. This senior agent told me that every day some high-level person in headquarters, or a SAC, was making a phone call to headquarters foreign operations section, or the Country Attaché, pushing for his guy or girl. And then, all of a sudden, the top five on the list had been completely reshuffled, only to be reshuffled the next day and then the next day as phone call after phone call came in. And there was nothing I could do about it.

So, it went. Needless to say, I didn't get Rome even though at one point I was, as least I had been told, number one on the list. And then, believe it or not, it got even more frustrating, if that was possible!! A few weeks after that, they posted not one, but two positions in Bern, Switzerland. I was sure to get one of these, right? So, I did the same as the first time. I submitted my name and my bio sheet and waited. Then I heard that I made the BQ list again. So far so good. Soon after that, I heard the same thing as before from the rumor mill – that I was number one on the list. But this time it was different as there were two positions open. If I was number one, I'd surely get one of these, right? Wrong. I didn't get it. I didn't get either one!

Then the floodgates opened. Paris opened. I didn't get it. London opened. I didn't get it. Vienna opened. I didn't get it. Milan opened. I didn't get it. Copenhagen opened. I didn't get it. Frankfurt opened. I didn't get it. Madrid opened. I didn't get it. I was beside myself. What was happening? What was I going to do? How could I get one of these jobs? That same senior agent saw my funk and tried to offer some support. He said that it was a process, that it could take a year or two, that it was important for headquarters to see the same names over and over so that they could see that the individuals applying were serious. He then told me that if it was so important to me, then

I would just have to stay at it and be patient. Truer words have never been spoken.

My supervisor at the time was Mike McManus. He was an incredible resource to have in my corner during this frustrating time. Not only had he completed a foreign assignment with the DEA, but since he had been involved in the process, he knew how the inner workings of how selecting the individual went. Almost daily he would come to me and ask which job I had put in for most recently, if that was where I really wanted to go, who did he need to call, etc. And he did. I would do the research and find out who the Staff Coordinator was in headquarters who was responsible for that country and who the respective Country Attaché was, and he did the rest. He would go back into his office and start working the phones. He made phone call after phone call after phone call.

What really impressed me about Mike and how he supervised his agents is that he had a very simple theory about managing his group. He believed that the four most important tasks were: keeping us all safe, getting us what we needed to do our jobs successfully (funding, equipment, training, etc.), getting us the promotions, awards, and accolades that we deserved, and lastly, getting our transfers — whether it be a foreign post like myself, or back closer to home, perhaps, for another agent. And, when I finally became a supervisor in 2017, I tried to do the same with my group and emulate him. Mike was amazing to work for.

Eventually, Brussels, Belgium was posted. I didn't know a lot about Brussels except that it was where NATO Headquarters was located and the seat of the European Union. So, I did some research and really liked what I read. It was considered the unofficial capital of Europe because it was so centrally located. It was also only a few hours' drive from Paris, Amsterdam, Aachen/Monschau, Germany and just across the English Channel from London. I was sold. I submitted my name. However, this time was a little bit different. I chilled out. I relaxed and just let the process happen. I let it come to me. I had decided not to stress out and let my name, case work, and reputation speak for themselves. Then a funny thing happened. All the stars began lining up. The Country Attaché was not only an agent that I knew, but he was the same agent who was stationed in the Bahamas in the Freeport office when I worked that case that I talked about earlier in this book where we seized 18 kilograms of cocaine. It was Steve Luzinski! My old buddy from the Bahamas. He not only knew me but had seen me work. He was familiar with an investigation that I had done and had seen my work ethic.

You can't buy PR like that. Also, by the time I had submitted my name for the Brussels spot, the SAC of the Miami office had been promoted to Deputy Administrator. And in DEA, that's huge as the Deputy Administrator is the number two guy in DEA, only behind the Administrator who is a presidential appointee. Effectively, the Deputy Administrator is the highest-ranking agent in the administration. And he knew of me and knew of my work. He was my SAC when I received the Administrators Award and was right by my side when the photo was taken. Of course, just as that senior agent had told me, the people deciding on the selection in headquarters **had** seen my name a lot by then, after all of the jobs I had put in for.

This time, all the stars were lined up for me. It was time. It was my time. Finally, I was selected for the Brussels position. Although it was just a lateral move pay-wise, my new title went from Special Agent to Assistant Country Attaché. Eat your heart out, James Bond!

The next step was language school – a six-month adventure that would take me to Rosslyn, Virginia for intensive French language training. Many people wondered why I needed to learn French for an assignment to Brussels and not Dutch, or Flemish which is a dialect of Dutch. It's a strange dichotomy. Belgium, which is about the size of Vermont or Maryland, is one of the few countries that has three official languages – Dutch (Flemish), French and German. It was incredible to hear Belgian citizens switch from one language to another as they spoke in a group of people. If you mark a line that divides the country of Belgium horizontally, it almost works out perfectly. To the north of that line is the portion of the country

116 – CHAPTER 21 - BRUSSELS, BELGIUM

that borders The Netherlands and you will find that the majority of people there are native Flemish speakers. And that the Southern part of the country, to the South of that dividing line, is where most of the native French speakers live as that is the portion of Belgium that borders France. There is a very small population on the Eastern border of Belgium, bordering Germany, who speak German.

But the theory that DEA held, as well as other U.S. Government entities, was that since most all of the Flemish speakers in the northern part of the country could speak excellent English and that many of the French speakers in the southern part of the country were not as accomplished English speakers as their fellow Flemish countrymen, that the language required by U.S. Government diplomats would be French. At first, I really didn't understand it either. But when I arrived, it made sense. The city of Brussels, the capital of Belgium, is primarily made up of Flemish speakers. And since Brussels was not only the capital of Belgium, the unofficial capital of Europe (many large U.S. companies have their European headquarters in Brussels), and the seat of both the European Union and NATO, they almost all speak perfect English. And this includes the majority of the Belgian law enforcement entities – the gendarmerie, police judiciare, prosecutors and judges – that the DEA and other U.S. Government agencies work with on a daily basis. As you venture farther south towards the Belgium/French border, this isn't the case necessarily.

The DEA and other agencies or corporations sending diplomats to work there for an extended period of time felt that if there was ever going to be a situation where their employees would need a language to get around, it would be French, mainly when they were working in the Southern part of the country. So, French it was.

I'd like to fast forward briefly to share a couple of funny stories about the language training. After I graduated from language school and had first arrived in Brussels, I was stuck for dinner one night. My household items were still being shipped so I had nothing to cook with and I hadn't had a chance to go to the grocery store yet.

So, I remembered seeing a pizza place not too far from where I was living as I drove around that day. I quickly ran out to get a couple of pizzas. As I stood there at counter ordering them, I was speaking in French and ordering in French. I ordered all of the toppings, sizes, side orders, garlic bread and drinks – everything in French. And as I was doing this, the person behind the counter was writing it all down without any questions or confusion. I was like, "Hot damn, this is incredible! This person understands **everything** I'm saying!" Just then, at the end of the order, he looked at me and said, "That will be about 20 minutes." **In the most perfect English!** He understood my French, which was great, but responded in perfect English.

This happened all the time and was frustrating to someone who had just spent six months in language school. I remember so many times being at a bar having a couple of drinks with my fellow agents or Belgian counterparts and going up to the bar and saying, *"Une autre bière, s'il vous plaît."* And then the person behind the bar responding, "Sure. Just give me a sec." It was almost comical.

The second story happened when I was first in country, and I would try to use my French as often as I could, naturally. Again, I had spent a long time in language school and the DEA had made a huge investment in this training as the entire school plus room and board was totally paid for by the DEA. That was a nice chunk of change after six months. One time I was talking to a Belgian counterpart in French and doing pretty well as he was understanding everything I was saying while we were bantering back and forth. He was a native Flemish speaker, but he was fluent in French. All of a sudden, he stopped me and, in perfectly crisp, clipped English, he said, "Keith, I speak perfect English so can we just talk in English?" We just had to laugh. I know I did. But what was I supposed to say? I mean, he was right. And French wasn't his native language either. I guess he would rather speak English than French, so we switched.

Back to language school. I left in January of 1998. It was a bittersweet moment. For one thing, I was departing to chase my dream. But I was also leaving my family and beautiful daughter who was only two years old at the time. It broke my heart, but it was what I had signed up for. Plus, my old Group 9 mates were really great and promised me that whenever a case dictated it, or if they needed me for anything, perhaps testifying in a trial, they would fly me back to Miami so that I could see my family and beautiful little girl. It was a very strange time in my life as I stated before. Besides missing my daughter terribly, it was actually a really nice break.

First, when we went to language school, it was all we were required to do. All of our investigations were reassigned, and we merely went to class each day and studied. That was really about it. But it made sense since there was little time to do anything else. A lot of people think that this was reminiscent of their Spanish classes in high school, or Berlitz, or Rosetta Stone or such. No. This was a six-month course – every day, five days a week, five hours a day, every month, for six months. This was the kicker – it was **total** immersion and one on one! Yes, that's right, *mon ami*. You walk in on day one, and they start speaking French to you. It was sink or swim, baby. As many individuals who had extensive foreign language training would affirm, it was the only way to become proficient in a foreign language. Thank God that I had two years of French in high school because some of my colleagues who didn't have any type of language training really struggled. Between school and studying every night, I was exhausted. Back to my point about case assignments. It only made sense that they got reassigned because I had very little free time while in language school.

Another thing that I found fascinating when I arrived was that there were about 80 agents like me going through language school when I arrived which just wrinkled my brain. That was a lot of agents and one hell of an effort on DEA's part. Talk about an investment in foreign operations! There were a lot learning Spanish, obviously, due to DEA's huge presence in South and Central America. And then there was a smattering of us agents learning French, German and Italian as well as agents learning Mandarin Chinese, Turkish, Creole, and even Russian, as we had just opened an office Moscow.

It was really impressive to see.

It was kind of like being back in college where every day we went to class, studied, worked out, and then did the same exact thing the next day. And then, again reminiscent of college, we would all get together at a bar or restaurant on a Friday or Saturday night (usually both!) and drown our sorrows and frustrations out over beers. We talked about the cost of living in Washington, D.C. (although we were all on per diem, a dinner in some of the restaurants in Arlington or Alexandria or Georgetown could cost us an entire week's worth of per diem!), missing our families or how our teachers were just going **way** too fast. Steve was there, too. He had gotten the Country Attaché job before I had gotten the Assistant Country Attaché job. So, he had started language school before I did, but we did overlap for a while. It was nice to see a friendly face once in a while and to know someone personally while I was there.

My frustration with my teacher was that he used to always say, "Remember this for tomorrow." after each task. Of course, I would write it down. By the end of a five-hour class I had a whole list if items that I needed to "remember for the next day." I would go home at night and study for four or five or six hours, whatever it took to complete those tasks. And then I would go into class the next day, and we would move right on to the next lesson in the book. Nothing was said about all the things I had to remember from the day before. No review, no questions about if I understood everything, nothing! This went on for weeks until I finally said enough of this nonsense. After that I was much happier and less stressed. And so, it went for six months.

One positive thing during that time was that crazy winter (1998) where the *El Niño* weather pattern affected much of the U.S. giving Washington, D.C. spring-like weather during the winter months. Every day it was in the 60s and was a huge break as I reminisced about the normal D.C. winters that I had experienced when I was a kid and living there for a couple of years while my dad served in the Air Force and stationed at Andrews Air Force Base.

Eventually, it was all over. I passed. A passing score with the DEA was a two out of a possible five. After scoring a two after three months, kind of like a midterm, I scored a two+ in my final which equates to a 2.5. Someone might be thinking that a two+ out of five is pathetic. But don't forget that a score of five is a native speaker, and a four would be a non-native speaker who was fluent. Obviously, those two scores were impossible for me to receive. Therefore, since a three would be the max, a two+ for me was a huge win, basically a 2.5 out of 3! In the end, it didn't matter. I had survived and had passed. And more importantly, I was done and going back home to Miami to pack out and head to Brussels to continue my adventure.

22
Arrival in Brussels

After returning to Miami, I was soon faced with another situation, a common one in the U.S. Government. We were low on funding. Since I had returned to Miami in June and the end of the fiscal year was always September 30, we were low on money. This was typical in the U.S. government, and I had been through it before. But this time it was different. Normally when that happened, all discretionary spending was halted and the only thing funded was operational costs. Since I had always been a street agent, as long as there were operational funds to cover my investigations, it never really phased me. Now it affected me since a move to a place like Brussels was not considered essential to the overall DEA mission. Consequently, I returned and waited for funding to come through.

What really frustrated me about this was that I had just finished six months of intensive French language training. And I returned to Miami, not exactly a mecca for French speakers. If I had studied Spanish that would have been great. I could go into any store, gas station, supermarket, basically anywhere in Miami and use my Spanish. Hell, I could have boned up on my Spanish just by reading Miller Lite billboards along the highway or listening to any one of numerous Spanish radio stations. But French was different. So, I buckled down and reached into my pocket and purchased a series of French lessons from a local teacher. We met once a week just to keep my French on point. It wasn't ideal and it was a far cry from five hours a day, but it was something.

To make matters worse, although this would help me in the end, the office in the U.S. Embassy in Brussels was empty at that time. In 1998 there were only two agent positions in Brussels – the Country Attaché and the Assistant Country Attaché. And both had just finished their tours of duty and had returned to the U.S., meaning the office was shuttered. It was just a coincidence that both had finished their tours at the same time. But, regardless, it was not a great look for the DEA in the U.S. Embassy in Brussels. This went on month after month until finally in November, the Deputy Chief of Mission, referred to as the DCM, and the true head of any U.S. Embassy around the world, made a crucial decision.

Allow me to backtrack for minute. Many people think that the U.S. Ambassador is the head of a U.S. Embassy, and he is technically, but these people are usually presidential appointees and just figureheads, whereas the DCMs are career U.S. State Department employees who usually run the show while the ambassador is out and about pushing U.S. interests with kings, queens, and princes. This DCM had to pass the DEA office every day on the way to his office. Finally, after months of passing a closed DEA office, he picked up the phone and called headquarters. He made no bones about his displeasure with the situation and told headquarters that if the office wasn't important enough to staff, funding issues or otherwise, then they should close it.

The next day, Steve, who was also waiting with me in Miami for funding after he had finished language school a few months ahead of me, was authorized to travel to Brussels for a 30-day TDY (temporary duty) to open up the office and provide a DEA presence in the U.S. Embassy. He was to return after 30 days and pack out for his permanent move to Brussels. At that time, upon his return, I would replace him and then do the same – complete a 30-day TDY in Brussels to continue the flow of operations until he returned for good. Then I would return to Miami for my permanent move to Brussels. Finally, there was light at the end of the tunnel! By the time these 30-day TDYs had been completed and I returned to Brussels for good, it was January, 1999 – seven months after I had completed language school!

But before I made the move to Brussels permanently, I had to complete that 30-day TDY. Again, my heart was torn since I was finally making progress in getting on with my assignment. Remember, it had now been almost a year since I had started language school, and I was chomping at the bit to finally get started with the actual assignment, but I had to leave my family and daughter again for a month, and that once more broke my heart. My only solace was that this was going to be 30 days and not six months, so I could definitely handle it. I just needed to stay busy.

I remember before departing Miami for Brussels to begin the 30-day TDY that I had to go to the local Nordstrom's to buy about ten suits, ties, dress shirts, and a few pairs of dress shoes. I had been informed that the U.S. Embassy in Brussels was one of the more formal U.S. embassies in the world since it, again, worked hand in hand with the European Union and NATO Headquarters. That meant at any time President Bush could be there, or Colin Powell, or Janet Reno, or Madeline Albright (I mentioned those individuals specifically since I got a chance to meet all of them). So, suits were mandatory when in the U.S. Embassy.... not just "no jeans" or business casual, but suits. Back home I went with my new attire and a credit card bill of about $1,000. And, these were 1998 prices.

President George W. Bush visits NATO.

Attorney General Janet Reno visits the U.S. Embassy in Brussels, Belgium. I am second from the right. Steve Luzinski is on the far right.

I finally arrived in Brussels to complete my 30-day TDY. The one nice thing was that I stayed in the actual house where I would be living when I made the permanent move. That was nice since not only did I have an entire house to myself instead of a hotel room where I'd lose my mind after 30 days, but it was the house that I would be living in for three years. This gave me a chance to bring as much stuff as I could with me in as many suitcases that they would let me take on the plane. It also meant that on weekends when I wasn't working, I could do a few house projects and get the place all squared away. Another nice thing was that I was alone. Although I missed my family and daughter like crazy, it gave me time to work long hours and get the DEA office up and running.

My days were spent reviewing case files, completing numerous case status reports since the office had been closed for so long, and meeting my Belgian colleagues that I would be working with for the next three years. These colleagues were primarily Belgian Gendarmerie Officers, the Belgian Police Judiciare, which was the investigative branch of the Prosecutor's Office, and the Belgian Customs Officers. I had the opportunity to meet my fellow U.S. law enforcement entities in the U.S. Embassy, in particular the FBI counterparts, and other U.S. State Department agencies.

I also took time on weekends to take long walks through the streets of Brussels. It was fascinating how old the city was. I explored all of the markets, the shops, the bars, and of course the famous *Grand Place*, the main square in the heart of downtown. It was amazing. I took advantage of the proximity to London since my sister was living in London at that time. One weekend, I boarded the Chunnel train which runs under the English Channel to spend a weekend with her and her family. It was an amazing experience.

After 30 days, my TDY ended, and I headed back to Miami. I had to pack out, put most of my furniture in storage since the house in Brussels was furnished, obtain diplomatic passports for everyone in the family, and get U.S. State Department physicals for the entire family as well, and complete a plethora of other tasks related to a move to the other side of the world.

I remember being so confused as to why we had to get U.S. State Department physicals instead of DEA ones as I had been given every year since I was hired on with DEA. I was informed that it was because all U.S. Embassies are under the U.S. State Department's jurisdiction and even though DEA would still be paying me and I would remain a DEA agent, obviously, I would actually be on a three-year loan to the State Department. Kind of like a temporary assignment. There was so much to learn!

One side note about the diplomatic passports that I found amusing was that **everyone** in the family received one! It was comical to see that my two-year-old daughter had her own diplomatic passport and full diplomatic immunity in case that finger-painting assignment in her pre-school class got out of hand! After all of those tasks had been completed, it was finally time to depart for Brussels for my three-year tour of duty. **Finally!**

One of the first things I experienced in Brussels was working in the U.S. Embassy. It was quite a sight to see from the outside. It looked like any other historic old building, but once I got closer, I could see the American flag flying high in the courtyard. The Belgian Gendarmerie were tasked with providing security on the outside of the embassy while the U.S. Marines were responsible for the security on the inside, manning Post 1. And the U.S. Ambassador's residence was attached to the back side of the embassy.

The one thing that was surprising was that, aside from the government offices housed inside, it resembled a small town. There was a post office, a hair salon, a snack bar, a cashier, a travel agency, a gift shop, and a convenience store. The convenience store even sold Shell gas cards which was a big help since back then gas in Europe was about $5.00 a gallon due to the crazy taxes in Europe but we, as diplomats and U.S. Citizens, were only required to pay for the gas and not the taxes which was what the gas cards provided. So, that was unique.

The other unique part of the embassy was a room called the bubble. This was where the 'country team' met once a week to discuss whatever was pertinent with the rest of the country team members. I rarely went to these since the participants were the heads of their respective offices inside the embassy, in this case, Steve, the Country Attaché. I would go once in a while when he couldn't make it, or when he was on vacation or travelling, and I found it fascinating. It was this tiny room that we could barely fit in, all sitting around the long, rectangular table. The Ambassador was never there as it was chaired by the DCM. When the meeting commenced, they would shut this gigantic door similar to a bank vault so that no one could eavesdrop from the outside. It was like we were back in the Cold War era. But I loved every minute of it.

The other great thing about the assignment was the travel associated with the job. I often had to travel to Lyon, France to attend meetings at INTERPOL, or to The Hague, The Netherlands to attend meetings at EUROPOL. Some meetings also sent me to Paris or Amsterdam or London to meet with DEA colleagues there in order to discuss investigations and possible overlaps with each other's investigations. By the time I arrived, the Schengen Agreement had just gone into effect. This meant that once inside the European Union, anyone could travel from country to country inside the

European Union countries without going through any kind of immigration checkpoint or customs offices. Basically, there were no borders. However, this allowed criminals to travel freely between countries, so it was important for the neighboring DEA offices to meet often because some of these criminals, investigations, and drug trafficking organizations had tentacles in numerous different countries. The Schengen Agreement was part of the whole European Union decision which not only dropped borders but also did away with each country's individual currency. As a result, there was no longer a Belgian franc or a German mark or the Dutch guilder as they were all replaced with the euro.

In addition to Brussels, our other main responsibility was the country (Duchy) of Luxembourg. We would also travel there once a month to meet with the Luxembourg Gendarmerie. Luxembourg-City was very beautiful but very small compared to other cities in Europe. It was known for its banking industry so most of the investigations that we assisted the Luxembourg Gendarmerie with were money laundering investigations.

As a matter of fact, we had this old DEA case from 1984 which was still open when I was there since a number of assets were still being processed and adjudicated in federal courts. Only later did I realize that this one particular asset in the investigation was approximately $200 million dollars that had been seized from a bank account in Luxembourg that belonged to Pablo Escobar and the Medellin Cartel. Back then, Escobar and the cartel were notorious for using banks all around the world, as well as offshore accounts, to attempt to try to hide their money. I was there in my office the day the check finally arrived in the amount of $200 million dollars payable to the U.S. Department of Justice. Escobar's accounts had finally been liquidated and the years of legal proceedings were over.

23

MLATs

As I settled into my new post of duty, the first thing I noticed in my day-to-day duties at the U.S. Embassy, and which would be a challenge for the entire three years that I was assigned to the Brussels office, was the difference in the legal systems. Compared to the U.S. legal system, they are night and day. Most European countries, including Belgium, use what is referred to as the Napoleonic code when it comes to law enforcement. As the term infers, it goes all the way back to the times of Napoleon Bonaparte, the famous French emperor. This code was enacted on March 21, 1804, and totally revamped the criminal justice system in France.

Eventually this same code was adopted by neighboring European countries, to include Belgium. Its original design was to protect citizens from overbearing governments and police states. One of the items included in this code is a term known as *Agent Provocateur* which translates to a "provoking agent," or in American slang an undercover agent. Basically, any type of undercover operation in these countries had to be tightly controlled and have approvals from the very top echelon of the respective law enforcement agency in that country.

To someone like me who worked side by side with other DEA agents who went undercover all the time and needed no other authorization other than the fact that the investigation warranted it, requesting permission from a group of Belgian prosecutors and judges was going to be a brand-new experience for me.

Additionally, the use of confidential informants in these European countries differed greatly than in the U.S. The DEA lived and breathed by the use of informants. It was our bread and butter. They were the eyes and ears on the ground. And we used informants in many different ways which depended on the individual at hand and the requirements of the investigation. Some were used for intelligence purposes only. Some were actively involved in making controlled buys of narcotics at our direction. It varied greatly. However, in countries like France and Belgium, they were used for intelligence purposes only. So, it was going to be a big change.

During my first few months in Brussels, I received calls from different offices back in the U.S. who, for example, had informants who knew traffickers in Belgium who had kilograms of cocaine to sell, or thousands of pills of ecstasy that they wanted to get rid of, so they were going to jump on a plane and fly right over to meet them with their informants. I was like, "Whoa, whoa, whoa. Hold on. That's just not the way it works here." And then I would go on to explain the whole Napoleonic code and *Agent Provocateur* laws. This was definitely going to be a steep learning curve. And I had to learn quickly as this was all new to me.

After hearing this, many people might wonder how justice was maintained and how investigations were initiated under these circumstances. That was another major part of my job during those three years – coordinating Mutual Legal Assistance Treaty requests or MLATs.

The best way to explain an MLAT is like this: Let's say that a federal law enforcement agency in the U.S. had an investigation, and although I was a DEA agent and assigned to the DEA Brussels Office, we were mandated to assist anyone from any agency with their investigations, from the DEA, to U.S. Customs, to U.S. Secret Service, it didn't matter. And this particular agency, during the course of their investigation, had found ties to Belgium or Luxembourg and wanted to do some kind of proactive investigation in Belgium using an undercover agent.

They would first have to start with their local prosecutor, usually an AUSA. That person would then contact the U.S Department of

Justice/Office of International Affairs, hereafter referred to as DOJ/OIA (sorry, the entire federal government was made up of acronyms). In turn, DOJ/OIA would then start coordinating with the Belgian Minister of Justice's Office, which was the equivalent of DOJ/OIA, of whatever foreign country was involved, in my case either Belgium or Luxembourg. A formal request for investigative assistance was then drafted and submitted in the form of a MLAT. That was the formal request used by both the Belgium and Luxembourg governments.

However, to make things even more complicated, other European countries used a request termed *Lettres Rogatoires* which translated in English to Letters Rogatory. And the word "rogatory" simply meant requesting information for an investigation. It was the exact same thing as an MLAT request, basically, but just a different term. And, as you could imagine, these investigations sometimes took anywhere from six months to a year to complete. It was a very lengthy process.

I remember that one of the DEA offices that I assisted indicted a Russian citizen living in Belgium at the time. The office and AUSA working the investigation requested through an MLAT request that the individual be arrested and extradited to the U.S. This process took an entire year to complete, and he wasn't even a Belgian citizen. But by the time the original MLAT had been completed, sent to DOJ/OIA, back to the AUSA for revisions/edits/corrections, back to DOJ/OIA a second time, forwarded to the Belgian Ministry of Justice, sent back to DOJ/OIA for revisions/edits/corrections, forwarded back to the Belgian Ministry of Justice......well, you get the idea.

So, after getting settled into my new house, learning this entirely new culture, getting to know my way around the U.S. Embassy, meeting the colleagues with the Belgian Gendarmerie, the Police Judiciare, and the Belgian Customs, educating myself on the MLAT process, and just surviving in a new country, a new crisis was gripping the U.S.

A new drug, 3,4-Methylenedioxymethamphetamine, better known as MDMA, or its street name of ecstasy, or XTC, was taking over as the number one drug threat in the U.S., especially among teenagers and young adults. MDMA is basically methamphetamine, which is in the amphetamine family, and commonly known as "speed." It's a psycho-active drug that is a Schedule 1 drug in the U.S. meaning it doesn't possess any legitimate function or approved medical uses. It was very popular in dance clubs and at "raves." Raves are clubs that would sponsor some popular DJ at the time who would then hold weekend long dance parties playing electronic dance music. Teenagers and young adults would flock to these raves and dance and take MDMA, among a plethora of other drugs, for two, three, or four days straight.

One thing that I learned right away while working in Belgium was that my daily life was going to be severely impacted by MDMA for the rest of my tour in Belgium. Just as this poison was gripping the U.S., I learned pretty quickly that the two main producers of MDMA in the world were The Netherlands and, you guessed it, Belgium. Almost all of the MDMA labs providing MDMA for the whole world was being produced in labs in The Netherlands and Belgium. It was mind blowing to me.

The scariest things to me were the labs and recipes. From all the intelligence that I was seeing come across my desk relative to the seizure or disruption or dismantling of these labs, I quickly discovered how risky the recipe for MDMA could be. I realized that these labs could be anywhere. They could be located in the backseat of a car, in a residence, a garage, or even mixed in a garbage can. And, as you can imagine, these labs weren't run by scientists in white lab coats. Also, there wasn't one recipe. Once the drug dealers included the primary ingredients, they could then add in whatever they wanted such as ephedrine, amphetamine, and methamphetamine to make the batch larger and more productive. By the time users were taking the drug in a club in New York City, God knows what they were ingesting!!

Another scary thing was that when the young club goers and ravers would take MDMA and dance for days straight, they would experience elevated body temperatures and dehydration. Because of the high the person was experiencing, he or she wouldn't even know what was happening to their bodies, sometimes resulting in death. It was really scary and I was in the center of the storm.

I tell you that story because it impacted the rest of my three-year tour in one way or another. On a side note, one of the perks of living in working in Europe was the travel. With the Schengen Agreement in effect and the ability to travel from country to country without hassling with customs officials and borders, along with incredible rail service available, I could leave Brussels and be in a number of prime European destinations such as Paris, London, Amsterdam and the like in a matter of hours. But that wasn't going to be the case for me. I was going to be doing a lot of traveling all right, but back to the good old U.S.A.

As I mentioned previously, the majority of the MDMA labs in the world at that time were located in both The Netherlands and Belgium. As is the case with most drugs in the world – cocaine, marijuana, heroin or, in this case, MDMA – the U.S. was the primary consumer. So, with those two points said, I found myself right in the crosshairs of a real crisis. My host country, Belgium, was the primary supplier, and my home country, the U.S, was the number one consumer. This didn't bode well for me, and my thought of exotic business trips along the Seine, or the Thames, or in the South of France vanished overnight. Here's what happened:

The Belgian Gendarmerie and Belgian Customs Service, doing their best to stem the flow of MDMA out of these labs and into their cities, did a full court press and started identifying these MDMA organizations one by one using whatever means they had at their disposal. And they were incredibly successful.

One of the full-court presses they did was at one of the express mail carrier centers in Brussels out near the Zaventem International Airport. They started seizing parcel after parcel after parcel containing anywhere between 10,000 MDMA tablets to 100,000 MDMA tablets. They would then do the best that they could to investigate the origins of the parcels, but every one of these leads resulted in a return address of an abandoned building, or a vacant lot, or the return address didn't result in anything. It was completely bogus. But they did have the recipients' addresses, obviously, as the recipients needed the parcels to arrive so that they could distribute the MDMA.

The Gendarmerie and/or Customs officer(s) would contact me at the U.S. Embassy to see if we wanted to take the parcels and travel to the U.S. in an attempt to deliver them and hopefully make the arrest. They were simply attempting to take the investigation as far as they could, and if they couldn't generate any type of valid investigation on their end, then maybe the U.S. could. Of course, the U.S. was definitely interested. This was a huge deal in the U.S., and at the time it was DEA's number one threat. In the case of an Internal Controlled Delivery, or an ICD as we called it, we would be providing the drugs. All the DEA office back in the U.S. had to do was to coordinate the delivery and then make the arrest. It was a huge opportunity for them. So, of course they wanted it. And as I sit here about to detail some of the deliveries and the details of these ICDs, often comical, I remember that never once in my three years, did I receive a negative response when I asked if they wanted the delivery.

But before I begin to detail some of these adventures, I need to explain just a little bit about the **process** without going into the weeds too much. We started with a seizure of MDMA from the express mail parcel. The Gendarmerie or Belgian Customs, whoever made the seizure, would start with their own investigation often ending in a dead end as I explained earlier. Then they would contact me and ask if we would want to attempt an ICD. I would first contact the DEA office that covered the recipient's address in their area of responsibility, what we called an AOR. They would then have to check with the prosecutors to see if they would be willing to prosecute whoever was eventually arrested after they had taken possession of the parcel containing the MDMA.

This was extremely important since there was no way all these hoops were going to be jumped through only to have the prosecutors tell us after the fact that they were too busy to prosecute the defendants, or that they were in a trial, or training, or on vacation. These **had** to be successful. In saying that, just like I stated that none of the DEA offices that I contacted during that time ever refused one, neither did a prosecutor.

Again, this was the craze in the late 1990s and these investigations with the amount of MDMA tablets involved made splashy headlines. The agreement from both the DEA office and the prosecutor's office came pretty quickly. Even this was challenging as this was still pre-internet, at least as far as a government agency goes in a foreign country in 1999. Also, to add to the logistical headache, Belgium is six hours ahead of the U.S. so a lot of these decisions came at midnight my time which was 6:00 p.m. on the East Coast in the U.S. But that goes with the territory.

At the same time, the Gendarmerie or Belgian Customs officers would be doing the same on their end with their hierarchy but in a different fashion. They were requesting that they be allowed to turn the parcel over to the DEA Brussels Office (me!) for an ICD to the U.S. And, obviously, I would have to have my DEA approvals and prosecutorial approval in place by then so that the release of the parcel could be approved.

The next step would be DEA headquarters approval since we would basically be importing an illegal drug into the U.S. I mean, it was pursuant to an investigation, but everyone all the way up the chain in the Foreign Operations Section of DEA Headquarters had to be aware of it, support it, and approve of it. The way this was accomplished was through transmittal of a DEA teletype requesting permission to complete an ICD. In this teletype, there were the usual questions that had to be addressed and answered mainly to do with the custody of evidence and security of the parcel. Believe me, if one of those parcels ever got lost, I would have found myself immediately reassigned to the DEA office in Djibouti (look that one up and you'll know what I mean!!). Basically, there was not going to be the standard checking of these parcels as checked baggage or put on a cargo flight. They were going to have to travel in the possession of armed federal agents. Once approval was granted, DEA Headquarters would issue me an ICD number. That made it official. But it wasn't over just yet!

We had to get the parcels there and not on a slow boat to China. This was an express mail service parcel. These parcels had to be there on time, usually in a day or two. And if we fooled around and took our time getting them there, the organizations receiving them would smell a rat and would just walk away from it cutting their losses instead of spending the next 10 to 20 years in Club Fed. They knew that these express mail services prided themselves on their guaranteed delivery promise, so if it was supposed to be there in a day or two and it got there in four days, they would know something wasn't right. So, we had a strict deadline to adhere to and we had to move fast. This meant only one thing. Once all the approvals were obtained and we had a green light, I would book a flight that same day or the next day at the latest, tuck my parcel under my arm and fly back to the U.S. to assist with the ICD instead of my dream of travelling to exotic places like Rome or Madrid.

24
International Controlled Deliveries (ICDs)

The first trip was to New York. Our Belgian Customs colleagues had intercepted an express mail service parcel with approximately 10,000 tablets of MDMA in it. As I mentioned earlier, they did the best that they could with working up the investigation on their end, but they were stymied almost immediately. The sender's address turned out to be bogus which shouldn't shock anyone. What drug dealer would put his or her actual return address on a parcel containing 10,000 tablets of MDMA? Not me. So, I received a call the next day from the Belgian Customs officials inquiring if I'd like to take the parcel and forward it on to New York for an ICD. While I was not crazy about a long transatlantic flight back to New York where, by the way, I had visited numerous times throughout my life since both of my parents were originally from New Jersey, I was excited for the ICD. I mean, 10,000 tablets of MDMA is a lot of pills!

The next 24 hours were a whirlwind of activity. As I mentioned before, the following approvals had to be obtained from the following before anything else: Headquarters/Foreign Operations, the New York office, the AUSA assigned to the Southern District of New York (SDNY), DOJ/OIA, and the Belgian Ministry of Justice. Once all of these approvals had been obtained, I had to complete a teletype to headquarters/foreign operations to request an ICD number. All of the aforementioned approvals had to be cited in that teletype and, most importantly, how we were going to transport the express mail service parcel and how were we going to maintain the custody of evidence for court purposes. There was only one way to do that. I would travel with the parcel never letting it out of my sight on a direct flight from Brussels to New York, with New York agents there to take the parcel from me the minute the door of the plane was open. And that's exactly what happened. I was on a flight the next day.

There is a funny side note to this story. Whenever I did these ICDs I would try to inform as few people as possible to protect myself and the integrity of the investigation. Obviously, the Belgian Customs Officials and the Belgian Gendarmerie at the airport in Brussels needed to know what I was carrying so that I could bypass the security line (this was pre-9-1-1 so TSA hadn't even been established yet). Otherwise, there would be nothing like having my express mail service parcel go through the x-ray machine with 10,000 tablets of MDMA in it! And then the pilot was always informed for obvious reasons. And that was it. I left it at that. If the pilot wanted to explain the situation to the co-pilot or to the flight attendant(s), that was his or her call. I left it at that and told as few people as possible. Well, on this flight the captain decided not to tell anyone else. It got kind of wonky from there.

I was seated in an aisle seat and the middle seat next to me was open. The express mail service parcel was under the seat in front of me so I could control it at all times. It was resting right at my feet, a perfect spot. The overhead bin wasn't an option because anyone who has flown a lot knows how many different people jump out of their seats and rummage through the overhead bin during the flight looking for a book or sweater or something. I just couldn't have that.

Right before we took off, a flight attendant stopped by my seat and noticed that I had the parcel under the seat in front of me, but since it was a fairly large parcel, it didn't quite fit all the way. She told me that it would have to go in the overhead bin. And here I was saying that it couldn't and, "By chance, did the pilot say anything to you about my unusual cargo?" She was not amused by this question and simply didn't understand why I couldn't simply place this parcel in the overhead bin especially since the one above me had plenty of room. I simply said that I couldn't do that and suggested that she speak to the captain. Tensions were starting to rise as she had no idea what I was talking about, where I was going with the suggestion for her to talk to the captain, and why the hell this parcel couldn't go in the overhead bin when there was plenty of room!

At this point, I quietly identified myself as a federal agent with the DEA and that I was on official government business and that I needed to speak to the captain. She reluctantly agreed, and we proceeded up to the flight deck – the flight attendant, my parcel, and me. You should have seen the looks I got from the other passengers. If only they knew what I had in that parcel!

When we arrived at the flight deck, the pilot remembered me and asked what the problem was. I calmly and politely explained the DEA custody of evidence policy as well as the fact that the arrival of this parcel in New York untouched was an integral part of an active DEA investigation. He then turned to the flight attendant and explained everything to her. Thank goodness! So, the three of us had us this little pow-wow right there in the cockpit. We tossed around different options but none of them could guarantee the safety and integrity of the parcel. Just then the pilot turned to the flight attendant and me and asked if the middle seat next to me was open, which it was. When we both responded that it was, he suggested that I buckle it in there next to me just as if it were a passenger.

Genius!! And that's exactly what we did. There I was in my aisle seat with my travel companion all buckled in nice and safe in the middle seat next to me. What a flight that was! I got some interesting looks! People couldn't imagine what could possibly be in that damn parcel! Anyway, the rest of the flight was fine although I really had to use the restroom before our destination. We eventually landed and proceeded to taxi to the gate and, sure enough, when the cabin door opened there were four agents waiting to greet me and take custody of the parcel. Thank God that was over! The delivery and arrest of the recipient took place a few days after that, so the investigation was successful.

It actually worked like clockwork. The group in New York that I worked with had an actual delivery uniform that they used in a controlled delivery that they had completed a few months earlier. So, one of the agents, acting in an undercover role, put it on, walked up to the residence, handed the individual the parcel, and arrested him. **Perfect!** And I returned to Brussels the next day and had a much more peaceful, enjoyable flight.

The next ICD I did was to Baltimore, Maryland. It was basically the same type of scenario. The Belgian Customs officials seized another express mail service parcel, however, this time it was much larger – 100,000 tablets of MDMA. We did the same routine as before. We first contacted the DEA Baltimore office, the United States Attorney's Office that represented the Baltimore office, DOJ/OIA, and the Belgian Ministry of Justice. Again, once all of these approvals had been obtained, a teletype to headquarters/foreign operations was completed requesting an ICD number. And we were off to the races once again.

I was on a plane the next day from Brussels to Washington, D.C., where I was to be met by Baltimore agents on the jet bridge with the express mail service parcel as soon as the plane door opened. It was funny because the **exact** same scenario with the flight attendant ensued. Once again, I had the parcel under the seat in front of me and wouldn't you know it, she started lecturing me about how it was sticking out too far from under the seat in front of me and that it would have to be put in an overhead bin. This time, however, I took a different approach. I simply said that I couldn't do that, and she was just going to have to talk to the captain as I had been given permission by the captain to store the parcel that way. I wasn't sure how she was going to take that but, honestly, I just wasn't in the mood to have a prolonged discussion with her about the parcel with all the nearby passengers listening in. And, luckily, she did just that. She said that she was going to see the captain and would be right back.

Well, a few minutes later she returned. I had no idea what to expect. To my surprise, she started apologizing over and over. She stated that she had no idea who I was and what I was transporting. She kept apologizing and I tried to calm her down and told her it was no big deal and there was no way she could possibly have known my mission. She ended the conversation by telling me that the parcel could stay under the seat in front of me and that she would make it up to me and that she had my back. What the heck did that mean? I would soon find out.

The flight went along fine without any other issues except, again, after a six-hour transatlantic flight to Washington, I had to use the restroom so badly by the time we landed. Since I was always traveling alone, I couldn't leave the parcel where it was and make a quick trip to the restroom. And there was no way to take the parcel with me. I mean, not only would that appear to be really suspicious as I'm sure the passengers would think that I was taking a bomb into the lavatory, but those damn airplane lavatories are so small I wouldn't have anywhere to put it down while I did my business. So, I held it. **Ugh.**

Well, I soon learned what the flight attendant was talking about when she said that she had my back. We landed and as we were taxiing to the gate she came on the intercom and made an announcement. It went something like this: "Ladies and gentlemen, can I please have your attention for a minute. We have an emergency on-board. It's nothing to worry about but when we park at the gate and the captain turns off the 'fasten seatbelt' sign, please stay in your seats until I instruct otherwise. That way we can take care of this emergency first. Thank you."

I was thinking that there was a medical emergency on board, or some kind of unruly passenger getting arrested, or something crazy like that. I was looking all around trying to locate the emergency as was every other passenger on the plane. Everyone was talking and looking all around, including myself! Of course, as soon as we parked at the jet bridge and the "ding" went off, everyone still jumped out of their seats and into the aisle to start retrieving their bags from the overhead bins. Well, this flight attendant came on the intercom again, madder than a wet hen. She was having none of it! Once again, she stated with a serious tone of anger in her voice: **"Ladies and gentlemen, once again we have an emergency on-board. It's nothing to worry about but please stay in your seats until I instruct otherwise. That way we can take care of this emergency first. Thank you."** And everyone sat right down and proceeded to look all around.

The looks on everyone's faces were priceless and reflected the same question. "What the hell is going on?"

Immediately after the announcement, I saw her scurrying down the aisle from the galley. I was really curious as to what was going on and where she was going. I was kind of wishing that I had my gun with me at this point since I had no idea what was going on.

I wasn't armed on any of these flights. I never traveled armed on any of the ICDs since I was traveling internationally, foreign country to foreign country, and carrying a weapon into a sovereign country was illegal. My weapon was locked up in my safe in my office at the U.S. Embassy in Brussels. Besides, all of the agents that I would be greeting at the door of any of these flights would all be armed.

Anyway, here she comes down the aisle, almost at a trot. I mean, she is really moving and means business. To my horror, she stops at my aisle and leans right over me and says, "Sir, let's go! I've cleared the aisle for you. You need to exit now!"

I remember responding, "What? Wait? That announcement was for me?" She went on to explain that she wanted to make it up to me, and that she wanted me to get off the plane first! She was only trying to help. **Wow!** Talk about trying to be inconspicuous and stay under the radar! That's the **last** thing I needed – unwanted attention. In an attempt to make this all go away quickly, I grabbed my parcel and proceeded down the aisle for the airplane door. I can picture it now as clear as it was that day even though that was about 20 years ago.

The other passengers were all looking at me and whispering. I can only imagine what they thought I had in that parcel – A note for the president? A beating heart? The Holy Grail? Who knows, but I was sure thankful to get off that flight! Within seconds the parcel was in the possession of three agents and a TFO who were waiting to greet me and take custody of the parcel.

The delivery and arrest of the recipient took place a few days after that, so the investigation was successful. However, it wasn't quite as easy as the arrest in New York. The recipient of the parcel had left instructions at the local express mail delivery office that he did not want the parcel delivered to his residence and to please contact him when it had arrived so that he could pick it up at the facility. We did so and took the parcel to the local express mail delivery office. Then we waited in the parking lot. One day turned into two days, and before you knew it, the third day was upon us. A lot of drug dealers did this to try to see if there were cops working the other end of it. They figured, "I'll be patient and give it a few days to pick it up" thinking that no cop in his right mind was going to wait for three days. These drug dealers never realized something. DEA agents are tenacious.

We **never** gave up or walked away. We would get the job done. I've lived it and I've seen it a million times. So, after the first day with all of us being up for 24 hours, we sent some guys home to get some sleep while we kept a skeleton crew at the local express mail delivery facility. We were just going to wait him out and take shifts. Eventually, they always caved in and came get their parcel. The greed factor kicked in and they couldn't take it anymore. They had to get those drugs on the street because that was a lot of money for them. Finally, at the end of the third day, he arrived and we promptly took him into custody. Damn, I was tired. And so, I returned to Brussels two days later after getting some sleep at a hotel and having a much more peaceful, enjoyable flight on the way home, once again.

Soon after, I was involved in another ICD, this one to Miami. It was the same scenario as usual – Belgian Customs officials seized another express mail service parcel, however, to be honest with you I don't recall how many tablets were in this parcel. Needless to say, it had to have been at least 10,000 tablets of MDMA to make it worth the while. Also, it was the same routine as before. We first contacted the Miami office, the United States Attorney's Office, Southern District of Florida (SDFL), headquarters/foreign operations, DOJ/OIA, and the Belgian Ministry of Justice. Again, once all of these approvals had been obtained, the teletype to headquarters/foreign operations was completed requesting an ICD number. Once again, I was back on a plane to the U.S. the very next day.

So, on this flight I was given the only seat that was left, the bulkhead row. Remember, since these flights were always booked at the last minute, there were very few seats to choose from. In this case, I had no choice. At the time of the booking, I didn't think anything about it. But when I boarded the flight with my parcel under my arm, I realized that bulkhead seats did not have a seat in front of them where I could stow a parcel, or piece of luggage, or anything else for that matter! And, as I have stated previously, I wasn't about to stow the parcel in an overhead bin. What was I going to do? **I was screwed!** Anyone who flies a lot knows that the bulkhead row is the first row. The first-class seats are right in front of that seat. I was starting to get pretty good at making these trips and figuring out the angles, so I figured that I would try something a little sneaky. I simply called the flight attendant over by hitting the "call attendant" button.

When she arrived, I just laid it all out there. I told her who I was and what I was doing as well as the contents of my parcel. I told her that the pilot knew all about it so she shouldn't be concerned. I then told her about the challenge of being in a bulkhead seat not giving me anywhere to safely store and protect my parcel. I said that I was more than willing to switch to another seat, but the flight was completely sold out. She looked at me with empathy but stated that there was no other option but to store it... I cut her off politely because I wasn't going to have another overhead bin story, and I asked very politely if there was any way I could move up to first class. I added that there was a seat available in first class as I could see it from my seat. I then explained that I could stow the parcel under the seat in front of me. She pondered it for a few seconds and quickly looked around, possibly to see if anyone was listening in or paying attention to our conversation. She responded with the most beautiful words I had heard in a long time and said that in this case, she would make an exception. *Now you're talking*, I thought as I quickly relocated. I did feel a little guilty, but hey, if I was going to make all of these flights and spend time away from my family, I deserved a little upgrade now and then. At least, that was how I explained it to myself. About an hour later, I was eating a filet with a demi-glaze, asparagus, and mashed potatoes. Ahhh...anyway...

The ICD went fine. No issues or problems. It was successful as they all were. The only bad part was on the flight back when I found myself in steerage with the normal, non-first-class folks. Oh well!!

25
250,000 MDMA Tablet Seizure

So, these ICDs continued for almost my entire three-year tour. I wasn't crazy about it, but what could I do? I was the only non-supervisory agent in the office. It was just one of those things. I had no choice. As I mentioned in the previous chapter, I even completed one back to Miami. I remember mumbling, "Seriously? I lived in Miami for seven years and of all places to go in the world I'm going back to Miami?"

I had heard about this school from Sarge, who said that this wasI did, however, get to participate in a pretty cool MDMA undercover operation. One of the main reasons I really enjoyed it was because it was a DEA operation in which the Belgian Gendarmerie would be assisting us for a change instead of my doing all of those crazy ICDs. Steve and I worked side by side on this investigation which reminded me of when we met years ago in the Bahamas. With Steve staying incredibly busy with all of the Country Attaché responsibilities, and me conducting all of the crazy ICDs, we really hadn't had a chance to work side by side since both being assigned to Brussels.

The case was initiated out of one of our California offices and one of the agents there, acting in an undercover capacity, had met a Belgian by the name of Dennis Maes. I'm not exactly sure how they met one another, but they did. Maes had bragged about all of the connections that he had in Belgium and that he could get the undercover agent any amount of MDMA that he wanted. After much negotiating, they eventually settled on 250,000 tablets of MDMA.

While these undercover negotiations were going on, two other agents assigned to the California office were in contact with Steve and I who were arranging for the completion/approval of the MLAT and case coordination with the Gendarmerie. This took approximately six months, but there was a lot to do during that time. There were numerous coordination meetings with the Gendarmerie in which the agents from California even travelled over to Brussels to attend some of these.

A funny note about these coordination meetings was that back then the Gendarmerie was **so compartmentalized**. We had to have separate meetings with the management and supervisors, then with the prosecuting judge, then with the case agents, then with the surveillance team, then with the technical operations team, and then with the undercover team. It went on and on and on. There was a new meeting each day. Damn, it was exhausting. I never really understood why they couldn't have everyone in one room at the same time. Do you have any idea how many times we had to explain the same exact operational plan over and over?

Finally, the MLAT was approved and the **entire** Gendarmerie was on-board and had approved the operation. The day of the operation finally came and honestly, it was relatively simple and went off without a hitch. Maes showed up at a pre-arranged location, a popular restaurant in Brussels. The undercover agent was sitting inside the restaurant in a booth when Maes arrived. Maes walked into the restaurant and located the undercover agent and proceeded to join him in the booth.

They engaged in small talk for a while and then got down to business. Maes said that he had the MDMA in the trunk of his car. The undercover agent said that he had the money in his car which was also out in the parking lot. The undercover agent then took control of the situation, which is of the utmost importance and pivotal in this case, and said that he wanted to see the MDMA first before getting the money.

If the undercover was going to see what he thought he was going to see, or shall I say hoped he would see, there would be no money needed. Maes would be cooked. And so that's exactly what happened. Maes led the undercover out to his car and proceeded to pop the trunk. And there were the 250,000 tablets. Unbelievable! The undercover agent said that he would be right back as he just needed to go grab the money from his car. As the undercover agent was walking away to his car, he gave the arrest signal. And, Maes was monkey-piled and arrested.

I remember thinking how easy it was. Not the six months prior, as that was grueling and a logistical nightmare, but the day of the arrest. Maes never argued with the undercover agent or demanded to see the money first, the normal back and forth banter and control game that is almost always present in drug deals. I don't know. Maybe it was because Maes considered the undercover agent a friend as they had been negotiating for the past six months and got to know one another very well.

The cool part about that operation was that, at the time, it was the largest MDMA seizure in Belgian history. I'm sure that record has been broken many times over since then, but it was a pretty cool feeling that day. It was a good day for the DEA, it was a good day for me as an agent **and**, most importantly, it was a good day for the U.S./Belgian relationship. It was the model case, in my opinion, of why we have DEA offices all over the world. This was the way it was supposed to work. This was the true meaning of international cooperation, diplomacy, and liaison.

I was coming into my third year of the three-year tour when disaster hit. The most horrifying series of events that ever happened to the U.S. took place, and I wasn't even living in the U.S. at the time which made it especially frustrating. And that disaster was 9-1-1.

26
9–1–1

"Para Bellum" If you want peace, prepare for war
– Marcus Aurelius

I was sitting in my office at the U.S. Embassy when one of my DEA buddies who was stationed in The Hague, The Netherlands office called me. He told me to turn on the TV immediately. I made a quick joke by saying that we weren't as fancy as The Hague office and that I didn't even have a TV in my office. He seemed really upset which wasn't his style as he was a really laid-back guy. He simply said to go find one and turn it on immediately. I remember saying to relax and that I would go find one when all of a sudden, he hung up on me! *What was the big deal*, I thought? Jeez! I then walked over to Steve's office and told him that we needed to find a TV. I remember him asking me why and me responding that I have no idea, but it sounded pretty important.

We walked downstairs to the cafeteria which was in the basement of the U.S. Embassy. We knew that something was up because the place was packed! Everyone was huddled around the TV, and they didn't look happy. As we got closer, I noticed that some people were crying. What the hell was going on? The people huddled around the TV quickly filled us in on what had happened. At the time, no one knew exactly the reason, just that a plane had crashed into the World Trade Center. Shortly after, the second plane hit. The room erupted in ghastly sighs and tears. What the hell was going on? To be honest, I remember thinking that the first plane had somehow flown way off course. Or maybe it was an Air Traffic Control (ATC) issue. But even so, if a pilot received directions from the ATC to keep flying right at a skyscraper, what pilot was going to listen and crash into a monstrous building? When the second plane hit, I was thinking about the odds and the absolute impossibility that this could happen twice. I mean, my mind was spinning. Then Steve whispered the word that we all were about to be very familiar with – Terrorists. I then realized what was happening. Our world had changed forever.

The next 24 hours were complete bedlam as we witnessed the other plane hit the Pentagon, and then United Airlines flight #93 crashed into a field in central Pennsylvania. Some people just stood there in shock with tears streaming down their cheeks. Others screamed and yelled at the TV. Others rushed home to take care of their families and check in on loved ones. Still others rushed back to their offices to phone friends and family members back in the U.S. Me? I have no idea. I have no memory of those hours immediately after the 9-1-1 attacks. I was just going through the motions. I really believed that I was in a state of shock. I was catatonic.

One of the most amazing things that I have ever experienced was the unbelievable outpouring of grief, emotion, sorrow, sadness, and most of all, love, expressed by the Belgian citizens. It was incredible. One of my neighbors at the time was a single woman. She only spoke French so our conversations passing one another in the yard, or on the street, were very limited. It was usually just idle chitchat. But I will always remember this moment. That night, after I had been home for a while and had spent hours on the phone checking on my parents and my sister, the doorbell rang. When I answered it, there was my neighbor. She was crying and had a **huge** bouquet of flowers. She just handed them to me and kept repeating, "*Je regrette, Je regrette, Je regrette...,*" which is "I'm sorry" over and over in French. It was so tender and sweet. I'll never forget that. And the rest of the country was the same. The outpouring of affection to anyone who was from the U.S. was just incredible.

But I had to go back to work the next day since the U.S. Embassy, as I had known it to be, was going to be forever changed. Our little slice of the U.S. was forever scarred.

The first big change was the concrete barriers put up all around the embassy. The location of the U.S. Embassy in Brussels was right along Boulevard du Régent, a main thoroughfare right in downtown Brussels. The fear was that a suicide bomber could drive a vehicle right into the embassy. The thinking was, hey, if terrorists did it with a plane...

The second big change was the Gendarmerie officers posted all around the embassy 24 hours a day, seven days a week. They would be responsible for the outside security of the embassy and the U.S. Marines, as they always were, would be in charge of the security inside the embassy at Post 1.

The third change was the parking garage. The new protocol was that when we arrived, we were to stop our cars and open the hood and trunk. A Gendarmerie officer would quickly check both for any types of suspicious devices like a bomb or incendiary device. Then the same officer would use an upward facing mirror mounted on a long stick to go all around the bottoms of our vehicles, again looking for a bomb or incendiary device. It was madness. Imagine the line of cars queued up trying to get into the parking garage since this procedure took about 15 minutes, and there was only one way into the garage.

The fourth big change was our country team meetings. These were usually held about once a week. Now they were once a day. And the only topic was keeping the embassy, the employees, and the Belgian Foreign Service Officers (FSOs) safe. Every embassy had FSOs. They were a huge asset since they worked in almost every department in the embassy providing translation assistance, cultural assistance, and a liaison between the embassy departments and the Belgian government. So, they were family to us. Anyway, the Country Team meeting was now led by our CIA and FBI colleagues who would update everyone on any threats to the embassy or U.S. businesses that had been forwarded to them by the intelligence agencies back in the U.S. To say the mood was dour was an understatement. We were on high alert every day and every night.

When I talk about this period of my life to some people, they say that they don't understand why a small European country like Belgium was so high on the risk list. I have to remind them that many large U.S. corporations had their European headquarters in Brussels, and more importantly, NATO Headquarters was located in Brussels which was a **huge** target of its own for obvious reasons. The bottom line was that anything with a U.S. flag flying on it was a target.

The embassy is still like that. A few years back, my wife and I went on a vacation to Brussels, Amsterdam, Paris, Brugge, and Monschau. When we were in Brussels, I wanted to show her the embassy, so we took a walk there one day. It brought back many sad memories when I noticed that the concrete barriers were still there. It broke my heart to go back to that God-awful day. It was gut wrenching.

Anyway, I tried to keep my spirits up around my wife. I didn't want to ruin our vacation. Luckily, something comical happened that made us laugh and took my mind off the solemn moment. She asked where my office had been located, and I pointed it out to her, an office on the second floor. I had a corner office so I could see it from where we were standing on Boulevard du Régent. I thought she was just going to look at it, so I started to walk away. Little did I know that she had decided to take a picture of it. **This was a major no-no.** No one was ever allowed to ever take a photo of an embassy. The guards, in this case the Gendarmerie, had no idea who it was, what country the photographer was from, the reason for the photos, or where that photo was going to end up. They didn't know if it was going to end up in a photo album or scrapbook at home, or in the hands of terrorists who were plotting to bomb the embassy and needed photos for their plan.

Anyway, as I was walking away, I heard the Belgian Gendarmerie assigned outside the embassy that day yelling at my wife to hand over her camera immediately because he needed to delete the photos. She was so scared and about to hand over her camera to the officer when I came running up. I quickly explained who I was as I showed him my DEA badge and credentials. I then explained that I used to work there many years ago and that the picture she was taking was of my office. When I said that, the mood quickly changed. A big grin came across his face, and he asked me if I wanted to see the office now and take a tour of the embassy. How cool was that! We immediately responded that we would love to, and that's exactly what we did.

Little had changed on the inside. Of course, the DEA office door was locked since it was a weekend, so we didn't get to see my actual office. But it was really cool to be walking around inside there once again, although my heart broke when I showed her the cafeteria. The TVs were still there and I remembered **that** day, that day all over again.

27
DEA Providence, Rhode Island

Some people ask why I went to Providence upon my return to the U.S. And my response was that it was the only office that had an opening in the entire New England area, and I wanted to get back to New England. So, Providence it was.

Another question also asked of me was why I only stayed three years in Belgium when I could have stayed up to a maximum of six years. Honestly, there were a few reasons. First, I personally found it difficult to live outside of the United States. I just did. I mean, it was great for a while, maybe the first year or so. Don't get me wrong, the traveling was fabulous. Well, other than the ICDs back to the United States! But I missed the small things. I missed an American cup of coffee instead of espresso all the time, or a U.S. newspaper instead of the International Herald Tribune, or ESPN instead of SKY sports, or watching the Super Bowl in real time and not dealing with the six-hour time difference.

Another reason was that I was a military brat. My dad was a Lieutenant Colonel in the U.S. Air Force for 23 years, so I had lived all over the world before I even started with the DEA.

Also, the job was changing. Any company or business constantly strives to improve policies and procedures. It grows and develops as technology improves. And three years away from that was a long time. I talked to an old DEA buddy of mine who had completed a full tour of six years at the post where he was stationed. He said that when he returned to the U.S., the job had TOTALLY changed. It was like he had to learn it all over again. He probably should have gone back to the Academy and learn the job all over again as a Basic Agent

Trainee, so I didn't want that for myself.

Lastly, as I stated a few pages ago, I was there when the 9-1-1 attacks took place and all I wanted to do after that was return to the U.S. to help in whatever way I could in order to try to heal the country. Again, being outside the U.S. when those attacks took place was really hard.

So, I returned to Providence in January of 2002. It was a **huge** adjustment. I needed to find a house first and foremost, so I spent the first three months living in temporary quarters looking for a nice house. The kids had to be put in school (my second daughter was born while in Belgium). I had to settle into a new office. I had to meet new co-workers and prosecutors. I had to find my way around, although we're talking about Rhode Island so that only took me a day or two.

This flurry of activity eventually calmed down. The kids were in good schools, and when we found a house, we purchased it. I was working with a good group of guys. Everything was going smoothly. Famous last words, right? All was well until one day the Resident Agent in Charge (RAC) called me in and said that he had received a call from the ASAC. He went on to tell me that the SAC of the Boston Field Division, in which the Providence office is part of, had a situation on his hands.

The RAC of the New Bedford, MA office had unexpectantly retired. No warning or two-week notice was given. Nothing. He just up and left. And the office was having some internal strife, so he wanted someone in there quickly. When the ASAC heard about this situation, she contacted the SAC and told him that she had the perfect person for this situation...**Me!** I should go back and explain something. This ASAC was stationed in Europe during the same time I was in Brussels, so the ASAC knew about me and my reputation. When the RAC mentioned all of this to me, I reacted with thanks but no thanks. I tried to explain to him that I had just returned to the U.S. and really wanted to re-learn the job and settle back in to being a regular street agent as I had done in Miami. I tried to tell him that in no way was I ready to supervise anyone and that it would be unfair to the employees who I would be supervising as well as being unfair to me. I added that New Bedford was about an hour from Providence and who would want that kind of commute?! He said he understood and would communicate it to the ASAC.

Well, he did, all right. The next day the ASAC called me directly and stated that the SAC wanted to see me first thing in the morning. Shit! So, I made the trip the next day from Providence to Boston which is anywhere from 45 minutes to two hours depending on the notorious Boston traffic. I spent the drive rehearsing my lines and trying to memorize all the reasons why this was a bad idea. I was confident that he would definitely see it my way. **Wrong.** It lasted about five minutes, actually more like two minutes. He said that I was his pick and to go there and straighten that ship out. He added that to make sure that I didn't take any crap. And he finished by saying to let him know if I needed anything. Great, just great! Just what I needed. The only good thing was that I would be receiving temporary supervisor's pay which I didn't give a hoot about, but at least it was something. So, I was off to New Bedford to be the temporary supervisor.

The first thing waiting for me when I showed up for my first day of work in the New Bedford office was a new car. It was a 2002 blue Ford Mustang. It was gorgeous. The office had received a couple of new cars, and this was one of them. The ASAC had decided to hold it aside until I arrived since I was really going out on a limb by assisting the office. The next thing that I encountered was the location of the office. It was inside a mall! The main office was being completely renovated and this space was temporary. But a mall? Seriously? They couldn't have found a better spot somewhere? Anywhere? And to make it worse, right across the hall was a mental health clinic. The patients were constantly getting turned around and confused and walking into our office. Also, we didn't have a janitor service, or a cleaning crew, or even a mailbox. Our mail got dropped off in the lobby/vestibule of the mall. It was a shit show, but I tried to make the best of it, settle in, and get to know the troops. However, I soon realized something. They hated one another. I shouldn't say everyone, but there were two definite divided sides that didn't talk to one another or even acknowledge one another. And this was where it started getting really bad.

I knew a couple of the agents assigned there and decided to go out to lunch with them to try and figure out what the hell had happened in this office to lead to such division. From what I heard, one of the other agents in the group disliked the supervisor after receiving a sub-par evaluation one year. Additionally, this supervisor recruited and then on-boarded a couple of new task force officers. Because of the recruits, the one agent thought that they were brought in to spy on him and keep tabs on him on behalf of the supervisor. Naturally, this agent decided to make the lives of these two task force officers a living hell. He would refer to them as rats and he even put a dead rat on one of their OGVs. This agent also recruited a couple of other people in the office to side with him and, in turn, the two new TFOs did the same. So, there it was. A civil war.

And what frustrated me was that I had to maintain operations. I had to keep this dumpster fire from getting out of control and keep people safe. I had to keep this ship sailing as the SAC had demanded. I did the absolute best I could. I didn't take any shit from anyone even though I was being pulled by that one agent to join his side. You see, although I had only spent a very brief time in Providence before moving over to New Bedford, as requested by the SAC, I did complete one investigation. It was a heroin investigation and, believe it or not, it was a joint investigation with, you guessed it, the New Bedford office. And the case agent for their office was this **exact** same agent. So, we knew one another. By not taking any shit, I'll give you one example of what I mean. I had to supervise these people. I had to keep operations going and keep people safe. I couldn't get involved in some juvenile argument. I couldn't take sides even if I wanted to. I had to remain completely impartial even though I knew some of the players in the game.

One day, those two new TFOs asked if I would like to go out to lunch with them. I said sure. As we were walking out the door, that one agent I was referring to came walking in. Strangely enough, he asked me what I was doing for lunch. I proceeded to tell him that I had already been invited by the two new TFOs but that he was more than welcome to come along. He looked at me and shook his head and simply stated, "It's starting already." Well, I knew exactly what he meant. He was referring to me and that I had joined ranks with them. I went to lunch that day, but I was **fuming** inside. My blood was boiling. Who the hell did he think he was? Anyway, I remember getting back from lunch and finding him in the office. I pulled him aside and promptly told him to never do that again. I stated that I'm my own man. I eat lunch with whoever I want, and I didn't need to check with him to see who I could or couldn't have lunch with. He got the point.

As the months went by, I had no idea but there was a plan in place to deal with these agents who were making everyone's life miserable. Unfortunately, no one decided to share it with me. And it all started like this. One day as I was driving into work, I received a call from a TFO. She was really frantic and explained that she was the first one in the office that morning and as soon as she arrived, there was a knock on the door. She said that she opened it up only to find three men standing there all dressed in dark suits. They proceeded to show her their badges and credentials and went on to explain that they were from headquarters and were there to conduct an emergency inspection of the office. What? An emergency inspection? I had never heard of that.

We did have an inspection division of headquarters and inspections were normal. **But** they were a huge deal and you knew about them months in advance. There was a **ton** of prep work to get done so an emergency inspection just didn't exist. I had been around long enough to know that for a fact. So, I told the TFO that I was already on the way and that I would see her soon.

I then proceeded to call the ASAC to find out what the hell was going on. When I explained the situation, she said that she had no idea. What? How did a team of agents fly in from headquarters in Washington, D.C. and the ASAC didn't know about it? Something really strange was happening. And it was going to get stranger, much stranger.

Although I had my suspicions, I went along with the inspection process. I was polite, courteous, and professional. I gave them whatever they needed, and I answered all of their questions the best that I could. Please remember that I had been there only for about a month by then. But something was really bothering me inside. I had been through inspections before. And this was not normal. The capper came when each inspector took one of the three 'problem' agents with them to separate locations for interview purposes. Interview purposes? That was not part of an inspection. And to where? An inspection consisted of inspectors spending long hours paging through case files with check lists to determine what discrepancies could be found. I then learned that each one had been taken to a different hotel room in the area. I remember thinking, *What the hell is going on here? This is the kind of stuff you see on TV.*

Anyway, I helped out the inspectors the best I could for the day even though I knew something wasn't right. The day finally ended, and the inspectors invited me to sit in on what they referred to as a close out meeting the next day, basically a session or meeting where they went down the list of what they found and how we should move forward to improve these issues. I agreed and was informed that the ASAC would be driving down from Boston and would be at that meeting, as well. That was a good thing because I wasn't going down with this ship alone. The inspection was a blood bath, and the ASAC should be here as well.

The next day came and we finally had the close out meeting. It was pretty bad. Numerous serious violations had been noted. Normally, if an office has one finding, which is basically an area in which **serious** issues were found, it's a pretty big deal and heads roll. Well, this inspection team found 14 findings! The only solace I could take away from this meeting was that none of this happened on my watch. I had just arrived. I sat there and bit my tongue still wondering what this was all really about. The ASAC, on the other hand, got an ass kicking. She was asked why there wasn't a cleaning crew? They asked why there was trash everywhere. They basically told her that as the ASAC, a GS 15, an *Assistant Special Agent in Charge*, she had **plenty** of authority to hire a cleaning crew. Anyway, she did not fare too well. As a matter of fact, she was demoted a few weeks after. Not fired but demoted to an ASAC job with far less responsibility. Needless to say, it was a long day. But things were going to get even crazier.

I don't want to get too far down a rabbit hole with this and do a deep dive into internal DEA policies and procedures, but some of the issues that led to the 14 findings were deemed pretty egregious to the point of being considered possible fireable offenses. And whenever that happens, the very next day Internal Affairs is at your door. And that's exactly what happened. These same three agents were now being investigated for possible offenses that could lead to termination. I had so many thoughts in my head that day. Why were these three agents being singled out? Surely there were other agents and TFOs in the office that contributed to the 14 findings, as well as the ASAC. Something just wasn't right. I could feel it in my bones.

About a week or two after the Internal Affairs agents had traveled to New Bedford and completed their interviews, the annual DEA New England golf tournament took place. I love golf and play all the time. To be able to play in a tournament instead of working, **plus** to know that all of the money raised went to great charities made it even better, especially when one of the charities was the DEA Survivor Benefit Fund. This fund collected and then distributed money to families of police officers and federal agents who have had a loved one, usually the father/husband, killed in the line of duty. The fund made sure mortgages were paid off, children went to college, etc. It was a very noble cause.

It was a great day until I received a call from the ASAC. I wasn't happy. She knew about the tournament, and she knew I was playing in it, and now she was calling me. I remember thinking that this better be good. I remember taking the call and hearing the following, "Hey Keith, sorry to bother you. I just wanted to let you know that the three 'problem' agents in your office have been transferred."

I inquired about where they had been transferred to as I was thinking somewhere else in the Boston division, maybe just to separate them from the other agents and TFOs in the office that they had been tormenting for so long. Lordy, Lordy, was I wrong.

She responded, "Eagle Pass, El Paso, and Calexico." I was shocked. I was speechless. And I didn't even know where the hell Eagle Pass was! I later learned that it was in Texas. I had never heard of agents being transferred to such remote places. I later learned that they were all on the border of the U.S. and Mexico. I was flabbergasted. She then asked me to let them know. And honestly, I really didn't appreciate that at all. Why me? I didn't have a dog in this fight. But I've always considered myself to be a good soldier. I remember telling her that if she wanted me to do it then I'd do it, although I thought that it was very unfair of them to put me in this position.

After I had informed the three agents of the transfer decision, which was met with utter shock and disbelief, the real drama started. One of the agents involved hired an attorney immediately to represent all three agents in fighting this decision. God knows what that must have cost. And one of the agents was relatively new on the job with a young family so I was not sure how he could afford legal fees.

But before continuing, it is important to know about one of the DEA's hiring policies known as the Mobility Agreement. I mentioned this agreement earlier. When new hires come aboard the DEA, they have to sign a Mobility Agreement which states that the DEA can re-locate them to anywhere they want at any time based on the needs of the agency. We all signed it. If we didn't, we didn't get hired. It was as simple as that. In this case, the DEA had decided to enact this policy. You might be wondering what legal case the agents would have against the DEA if the mobility policy was simply being enforced. The agents, through their attorney, claimed that it was a punitive move, or a disciplinary move. They felt that the DEA, specifically the SAC of Boston, issued the transfer order based on their role in the unrest at the New Bedford office over the past six months.

I could see both points. I obviously knew about the Mobility Agreement my entire career, but I had never seen it used in this manner. Actually, the **only** time I ever saw it used was when I was in Miami. And that was when the DEA had decided to transfer a bunch of agents who were hired in the Miami office, stayed in the Miami office, and had never left it. They had been there for years without ever having to make a transfer. So, they took this handful of agents and transferred them to other offices around the country that were either in need of people because of being short staffed, or the office in question needed senior agents. This clearly wasn't the case.

I tried to go about my business and keep the New Bedford office afloat and operating, but it was difficult. As hard as I tried to stay out of the drama, I kept getting pulled back in. As the lawsuit progressed, the case was presented to the Merit Systems Protection Board (MSPB) which is a pseudo court system for federal employees who believed that they had been subject to certain unfair practices like suspension, demotion, wrongful termination, or retaliation. And, obviously, the DEA, like in any other judicial matter, had to prepare their case. And prepare witnesses. You guessed it. They wanted me to be their star witness.

Attorneys from the DEA Chief Counsel's Office in headquarters interviewed me over the phone, not once but twice. Then I was called up to Boston on a Friday night, of all times, to meet with a DEA attorney who had flown in for the day. And it was incredibly frustrating to me because they kept trying to get me to say things about the agents that just weren't true. Maybe it was true, but I had no knowledge of it. I barely knew these guys. And time after time after time, they kept trying to put words in my mouth. They would ask me the same tired questions such as, "Wouldn't you say they hated authority?" or "Name a time they disobeyed a direct order?" And I would answer that I had no idea if they hated authority because I had just started in this office and that they had never disobeyed anything I ever said.

It was really unfair because I could see and sense their frustration with me by not telling them what they wanted. The bottom line was that in all my years of testifying in state, federal, and international courts, I have never ever lied on the stand under oath, and I certainly wasn't going to start now. It was simple. Anyway, as the MSPB hearing edged closer and closer, I was informed that I wasn't on the witness list anymore. Thank God. I just wanted to be left alone and return to Providence as soon as I could and put this temporary assignment in my rear-view mirror. But I couldn't just yet. Things were going to get real.

I remember that when the MSPB proceeding started, I was working in Providence that day as I still would go there occasionally to clean up some of my cases. While there, I received a call from the ASAC. *What now*, I thought?? Believe it or not, I was informed that I was back on the witness list and that I should get my suit on (most agents kept a suit at the office just for situations like this – when they get a last-minute notice that they're needed on the witness stand) and start driving to Boston. This was not what I needed to hear. But, again, ever the good soldier, I did as I was told. Things were about to get bizarre.

At about halfway into my drive to Boston I got **another** call from the ASAC telling me that Chief Counsels Office decided at the last minute that they didn't need me and that I could stand down and return to Providence. What a cluster fuck! I immediately exited the highway and turned around and started heading back south on I-95.

Wouldn't you know it? Yes, I received yet **another** call from the ASAC telling me that since Chief Counsel's Office had taken me off the witness list, the defense counsel added me to their witness list!

I was going to be a defense witness **against** my own agency, **against** the DEA. Apparently, when I was taken off the DEA witness list, the defense counsel smelled a rat and figured that they weren't going to use me for a reason and that reason must be because I didn't have anything damaging to say about their clients. They were right. Once again, I turned around and headed to Boston. I was literally sick to my stomach at this point and nauseous from driving in circles.

I got there eventually, parked, and went into the courthouse. I proceeded to check in and waited to be called in to the witness stand. Eventually, I was asked to enter the courtroom where I was sworn in and then seated in the witness stand. As you can imagine, I was asked the exact same questions about the three agents that I was asked in the witness prep conversations with the Chief Counsel's Office since they had predicted that the answers would shine a good light on their clients. And to their credit, they were right.

In the end, believe it or not, the MSPB judge sided with the DEA citing the Mobility Agreement. The judge stated that although the policy was not usually used in that manner, in turn, the policy didn't say that it couldn't be used in that manner. This was just a summary of the decision as the entire decision amounted to a 90-page document. But that was the crux of it.

And so, the agents were transferred to Eagle Pass, El Paso, and Calexico respectively. One final part of this bat shit crazy story that I couldn't leave out was that one day I received another call from the Boston office but directly from the SAC this time. And during this call he asked me if I could drive to Boston for a meeting with him. Another drive to Boston, but what could I say? After all, he was the SAC! And, it was on DEA time and, of course, as always, I would be using my OGV so it wasn't all bad.

When I arrived and met him, we chit chatted for a while. Then he proceeded to thank me for everything that I had been put through and how much he appreciated it. He then said that I could return to the Providence office and continue with my tour of duty there and that he would rotate another senior agent in from another office to be the new temporary supervisor in the New Bedford office which was fine with me. I had done my time. He then added that the vacancy announcement for the new supervisor of the New Bedford office had just been posted and that if I wanted it, he could guarantee that I would get it. I thanked him and politely declined, thinking that I wanted nothing to do with that slog again! What a nightmare that was!

28
DEA Cincinnati, Ohio

In 2009, I completed a voluntary transfer to the Cincinnati, Ohio office. I did this in order to be closer to my present-day wife who was from Columbus, but Cincinnati was the only office in the area with an opening. We both had children from another marriage, but her divorce decree stated that she was not allowed to re-locate outside of Ohio due to shared parenting with her ex-husband. So, Cincinnati it was!

When I first arrived in Cincinnati, there was a scourge going on that I was completely unfamiliar with. It was pain medication and the existence of 'pill mills.' Pill mills were pain medication clinics staffed and run like any other urgent care facility or doctor's office. And these were real doctors who worked in these pill mills. But the difference was that these doctors had a dark side to them. More on that later. I soon learned that Ohio was the epicenter of these pill mills. If one was to drive down to the Southeastern part of the state, they would see these pill mills, one after another. It was sad. And they were packed! People would line up first thing in the morning hours before the office had even opened. The line would wrap around the building and into the parking lot.

They would drive to Ohio from places as far away as Florida because no one had cracked down on these pill mills in Ohio yet as they had in other parts of the country. Ohio was still fertile ground. The reason they were so popular was because they provided quick and easy access to oxycodone or Oxycontin, which is the brand name for oxycodone. Doctors were prescribing these drugs like candy without any type of check-ups or evaluations. All anyone needed was an MRI and CASH, cold hard cash. And it didn't matter if the person had health insurance or not because they didn't take it, just **cash**.

You see, this is what I was referring to before. The doctors were rogue doctors and only interested in one thing. **Cash**. And lots of it. 'Patients' could go in with an MRI of a dog's skull and as long as they had cash, the doctors would prescribe Oxycontin to them. No check-up, no evaluation, and no questions asked. It was similar to a crack house. Patients would line up, wait their turn, finally get in, and after about five minutes, they would come walking out with their prescription. These pill mills would see hundreds of patients a day.

One of the first things I learned is that Oxycontin is a derivative of morphine, the same as heroin. To make it simple, Oxycontin is legal heroin, a painkiller. What made it worse was that a lot of these pill mills were also dispensaries, meaning that they would fill the prescription in the same facility just like a pharmacy. No need to go anywhere else. One stop shopping at its best. And these people were so anxious for their high that when they finally received it after waiting in line for hours, they would get in their cars and literally grind it up on the dashboard of the car and snort it. I saw it many times on surveillance!

The Cincinnati AOR covered this southeastern part of the state. That's how we got involved. There were so many complaints about these pill mills and overdoses that we had to do something. But what was frustrating to me, as I was the lead agent, was how to go about investigating them. I mean, the doctors had medical licenses, and it was not illegal to charge cash.

But how could we gain access inside one of these places? How could we actually get inside the examination room? Then one day it came to me. We would have to treat it like any other investigation, just like a crack house or a buy-walk operation. We would first have to find a suitable undercover agent. Then we would have to somehow get our hands on a bogus MRI. Next, we would wire that individual up with a recording device so that we could hear what was going on outside in our cars on surveillance. That way we would be able to know if there was something wrong and would be able to make entry and extract our undercover agent.

And that's exactly what we did. We found an undercover agent and were able to get our hands on a bogus MRI (we were working the investigation as a joint investigation with both the Ohio Medical Board as well as with the Ohio Pharmaceutical Board, so getting a bogus MRI wasn't an issue). We then wired up the undercover agent and gave him/her a certain amount of Official Authorized Funds (OAF), or 'buy money.' And then we sent the agent in. Over and over. We made numerous controlled buys until one day we raided the pill mill with a federal search warrant and shut the clinic down – for good. And we were able to arrest both the owner and the principal physician. It was a good day for the good guys. It was very rewarding to be able to shut that down.

The only drawback to all of this was that if you took away a person's high and they were truly addicted, they would find another way to get it. And what happened was that as these pill mills were shut down one by one, they flocked to Columbus, Ohio. The reason for this was that the majority of the west side of Columbus was Mexican and there was a good supply of heroin coming in from Mexico. I was not sure why or how this happened, but it did. It was similar to Minnesota which had a large population of Somalis. Being a Mexican heroin trafficker meant that they could get incredibly cheap and super potent heroin straight up from Mexico. Remember that Oxycontin is basically heroin. So, I always referred to it as the perfect storm. We had this large number of people who were addicted to Oxycontin, and all of the pill mills had been shuttered. But just a couple hours away, Columbus had super powerful heroin at very cheap prices. Ultimately, the two met!

29
DEA Columbus, Ohio

"Once more into the breach, dear friends, once more."
– William Shakespeare (King Henry in Henry V)

After two great years in the Cincinnati office, I had a chance to transfer to the Columbus office. An opening was available after one of the agents assigned there was granted a voluntary transfer to the Little Rock, AR office. I was ecstatic! The reason why this was so important to me was because I lived there!

As I touched on before, when I re-located to Ohio, the only office Ohio anywhere near Columbus that had an opening was in Cincinnati. I took it just to get into the division knowing that once I was in it, it would be a lot easier to move around. But my wife lived in Columbus and couldn't move because of her son. That meant that I had to drive back and forth every day between Columbus and Cincinnati. It's normally a 90-minute drive which was bad enough. However, the DEA had a rule that we could only drive our OGV 50 miles from home to work and return. Obviously, if every agent in the DEA got an OGV, that was a lot of gas. I could understand why this was enacted. Consequently, I was forced to park it halfway between Columbus and Cincinnati and use my personal car the rest of the way. But where? At that time, we owned a boat which we kept in an indoor storage facility to protect it from the elements. So, I simply rented another unit next to it at $100 a month and stored my OGV in there overnight. I would get up each morning and drive to the halfway point, Wilmington, Ohio, in my personal car. Then pull my

OGV out of the storage unit and park it on the side. I would then pull my personal car in the storage unit. Finally, I would get in my OGV and drive the rest of the way to work in downtown Cincinnati. And then repeat the whole process after work. I used to call it planes, trains and automobiles!!

Then someone mentioned to me that equal distance off the highway in the other direction was the Wilmington Police Department and that I should check the parking there. The person mentioned that I should ask if maybe they would let me park in their parking lot. It would at least save me $100 a month. I figured that I could at least try. I mean, at worst, they would just say no. One day I drove to the police department and met with the Assistant Chief. He informed me that I could park in the lot and that they would keep an eye on my car overnight as they had a 24-hour dispatch center which monitored cameras all over their facility, including the parking lot. I was so happy.

The drive was brutal enough, but this would give me piece of mind that the OGV was safe and secure. Plus, it was going to save me $100 a month. And did they treat me well! I remember one morning pulling in with my personal car after getting six inches of snow the night before, and the Assistant Chief was out there brushing the snow off my OGV! What an incredible person! When I finally received my transfer to Columbus, I went to a local restaurant in Wilmington and bought him a gift card for him and his wife. It was the least that I could do!

I enjoyed being home in Columbus and settled into my new group quickly. I was assigned to the Southwest border initiative. As I stated earlier, the west side of Columbus was predominantly Mexican, so we focused our intentions on these traffickers and the heroin that they were selling. Again, the heroin supply was endless, and it was some of the purest heroin anyone had ever seen.

We tried to do the best we could and not let the heroin hit the streets of Columbus while also trying to move up the chain of command of whatever organization that we were after at the time.

One of the agents in the group at the time was a smart, talented, hard-charging agent by the name of Tim Reagan. He was one of the best agents that I ever worked with. Tim came up with the idea of initiating surveillance at different hot spots around the west side of Columbus. We would start at places like convenience stores, gas station, and local markets. We would pick a different spot each day. And we would sit and watch and wait.

Almost daily, we would see the same routine. Eventually a car would arrive, but the driver wouldn't leave the car to enter the establishment and would just sit there. That was our first clue. We knew we were on to something. I mean, how many times does anyone drive to a convenience store or gas station and then just sit in the car with the engine running? To make the situation more suspicious, within a few minutes another car would arrive. Then one of the individuals, usually the buyer of the heroin, would get out of the car and walk over to the seller's car and get in. Seconds later, the buyer would exit, get back in his car and leave. At that point we knew that the heroin transaction had been consummated.

We would then pull the vehicle over as soon as it left the area. Sometimes we wouldn't even have to pull the vehicle over. The individual would pull over immediately and start injecting the heroin. I mean, they just couldn't wait. It was sad to see. I remember pulling one female over, and she started shoving all of the tiny balloons of heroin (heroin dealers will often use pieces of balloons to tie the heroin in) into her mouth and trying to swallow them! We were trying to pull them out of her mouth for her sake (if one of these had burst in her stomach that would have been almost a certain death) and for our sake as that was evidence.

The idea was to tell these individuals that they were going to go to jail that very minute unless they decided to cooperate with us. They could make a phone call to the same person the next day, a phone call that was supervised and recorded by us and set up another heroin transaction. If they agreed to do so, we would start the entire "jump out' routine all over again the next day, but **this** time we would grab the seller. And we would do the same routine over and over, taking our investigation up the chain as far as we could.

After doing these heroin cases and being in Columbus for a couple of years, and also completing a stint at the Columbus International Airport interdicting flights, I was called into my supervisor's office. He wanted to know if I would accept a temporary assignment to the FBI office in Columbus. At first, I was baffled but intrigued. This happened all of the time with local police departments and the TFO program that I described earlier in this book. This, on the other hand, was quite unusual and very rare. So rare, in fact, that I had never heard of it being done between two federal agencies until now. So, I wanted to know more.

Basically, it was pretty simple. Columbus was a relatively small city and it only made sense that the DEA and FBI offices in that city worked together and not fight one another. I immediately accepted for a few reasons. First, it was the FBI. How cool would that be? I mean, I bled DEA. It was my home agency, my family, and it was near and dear to my heart, but the FBI has such a glorious history. Second, it would be a nice change of pace. It would be something different as I had been with DEA for 22 years at that point. And, finally, and probably the most important reason was that an arrangement like this was important and critical to federal relationships.

I had seen the in-fighting between the DEA and FBI for years and I **hated** it. One of the reasons was that enforcing the drug trafficking laws, basically the Controlled Substance Act (Title 21), was all that the DEA did. The DEA enforced one U.S. code, and that was Title 21. The FBI, in turn, enforced 108 different codes. Of course, 99.9% of their time was spent on the biggies like terrorism, white collar crime, health care fraud, corruption, etc. But one of these is drug trafficking. They have always refused to let that one go and just let the DEA handle it as we were the experts world-wide. We were always tripping over one another, and it often led to in-fighting. I hated it.

This way, I could work for the FBI while I coordinated their cases with the DEA. I would be a liaison officer between the two, something which I was good at after my tour in Brussels. I took him up on the offer immediately! I would still be a DEA agent and get paid by the DEA, but I would report to the local FBI office instead on a daily basis. Oh, and he mentioned something quickly as I left his office, that they (FBI) were "just starting a pretty cool gang case."

30
Short North Posse (SNP)

When I reported to the FBI on my first day, I met everyone, exchanged introductions, and proceeded to move into my new desk. I then met my new supervisor who was really nice to me. We chatted for a while and after a bit, he mentioned that he would make an appointment for me to get my FBI credentials. I was a little taken back by this as I had DEA credentials. He then explained that since they investigated more than just Title 21 codes and mostly Title 18 codes, I would have to be deputized as a Federal Task Force Agent and receive FBI credentials. How cool was that? And I eventually did. I figured I must have been one of just a few federal agents at the time with dual deputizations and credentials.

I then met with my new group – the FBI Safe Streets Task Force, which, basically, was a fancy phrase for the drug unit. It was then I learned about this new case that they had recently initiated. It was a gang case that was targeting the Short North Posse, or the SNP. I remember thinking how cool that sounded. Then it got better. Within this gang was a sub-group who called themselves the Cut-Throat Committee, or Homicide Squad. They were the enforcers of the group. The Short North is an area of Columbus that is just "north" of downtown Columbus and just "short" of Ohio State University's campus. This gang lived and operated in the Short North area. I was hooked at that point. I remember thinking that this was going to be a really interesting assignment. I couldn't have been more correct.

Initially, the investigation started with some strategy meetings with the investigative team. The investigative team included two very skilled and highly regarded prosecutors from the U.S.

Attorney's Office – Dave DeVillers and Kevin Kelley, four detectives from the Columbus Police Department – two from the gang unit and two from the homicide department, one FBI agent, one agent from the Alcohol, Tobacco and Firearms Agency (ATF), and one detective from the Franklin County Sheriff's Office. It was a pretty complete team.

I soon learned in these first meetings that this was the third wave of the SNP. It was a family organization. The first wave was the original wave during which the SNP was dismantled in 1995. At the conclusion of that investigation, more than 40 members were arrested and tried. However, soon after that, the sons and other relatives of these original SNP members took over. Then in 2006, 10 of these members were arrested, then 19 more in 2010. But they kept resurging. Law enforcement needed to cut off the head of the snake.

As our strategy meetings continued, I learned another thing for which I need to take some time and outline as you will see how this comes full circle by the end of the book. The leader of the SNP at the time was an individual by the name of Robbie Long. I had to chuckle during this meeting and hearing Long's name.

I had actually arrested Long years before, in 2011. It was a Controlled Delivery of 700 pounds of marijuana from El Paso to Columbus. Again, just like in the Lord investigation, a Controlled Delivery is where the drugs have already been seized pursuant to an arrest or delivered to an undercover agent. In this case, the El Paso office had an undercover agent that had infiltrated a large drug trafficking organization (DTO) that operated between El Paso and Mexico. And this undercover agent had touted himself as a transportation broker who could deliver any amount and number of drugs anywhere in the country safely and securely. For a price of course. The undercover agent had convinced the DTO that he had a network of cars and trucks that could guarantee delivery anywhere the DTO needed it. The undercover agent would organize the transportation and then deliver it to whoever the DTO wanted. All the undercover agent needed were the drugs and a contact number.

The undercover agent would do the rest. And so, it was.

The undercover agent took possession of the drugs, in this case 700 pounds of marijuana. And the undercover agent was given a phone number to contact when he arrived in Columbus. Little did the DTO know that within a day or two, the drugs were loaded onto a DEA aircraft and flown to Columbus for the delivery. And on the day of the delivery, my office in Columbus, after formulating a complex and detailed plan of delivering the drugs, made the phone call. We had rented a Ryder truck and we had installed a GPS unit on the truck so that we would know where it was at all times. We were ready.

Long showed up with a couple of buddies and after a few minutes of negotiating with the undercover agent (he had flown up with the drugs on the DEA aircraft), the keys of the truck were handed over to Long. As they departed, we had numerous vehicles in waiting to conduct surveillance. We also had a different DEA aircraft in the air assisting with the surveillance.

These things happened in law enforcement, and after suspecting that they were being followed, Long and his crew ditched the truck and started running from us. It was a cluster fuck at the time but eventually, after a foot chase, we caught all three and they were arrested. That will get your heart pumping!

Back at the office, while we were booking and processing all three individuals, Long refused to cooperate or talk to us **or even give us his name**. He refused to say a word. At the time, we had no idea who he was or who we had arrested. It was only after a couple of days did we know that it was Long. And that was only because his fingerprints had come back from the FBI confirming so. I remember colleagues from the Columbus Police Department calling me and congratulating me because we had arrested Long who was the leader of the SNP at the time. To be honest, I had no idea what the SNP was then. I didn't even know what it stood for.

Long eventually pled guilty and was sentenced to seven years' incarceration. We thought that would be the end of Long, but he continued with his reign of terror from inside his prison cell. It would lead to a moment that I would never forget. Enter Karen Fitz, Long's long-time girlfriend.

As stated previously, the federal prison system is run by the BOP (Bureau of Prisons). After a defendant pled guilty and was incarcerated and then finally sentenced, he was sent to a permanent BOP facility somewhere in the U.S. But this process could take anywhere from six months to a year. And in the meantime, the defendant was housed at a local jail. In Long's case, it was the Franklin County Jail in Columbus. At that time, we had a detective with the Franklin County Sheriff's Office assigned to the DEA Task Force who had started his career with the Sheriff's office working at the prison. He knew that all of the phone calls that the inmates were allowed to make at the jail were recorded. And he also knew that even though there was a long preamble at the beginning of each call informing the defendant that they were being recorded, they **still** said some incriminating stuff on the phone, or talked too much and revealed a part of the DTO. They said stuff like, "...well, they got me but at least they didn't get that $100,000 back at my crib." It happened. Seriously.

This detective went to the prison a couple of weeks after Long had been incarcerated and had all of his phone calls downloaded onto CDs. And for the next week or so, he was consumed with listening to these calls hoping for a break. He finally found one, but it was not what we had expected at all or hoped for as it led to a heart-breaking tragedy.

It involved a phone call between Long and his girlfriend, Karen Fitz. Long was heard telling Fitz to put "30" aside and to give it to Jerry. We knew immediately who this was as Jerry represented Long in the court proceedings following his arrest. And we deducted that the "30" had to be in reference to $30,000 being set aside to pay Jerry his legal fees for representing Long. Suspecting that this was drug money, we raced out to Fitz's house after quickly searching different databases for her address.

When we arrived, Fitz was there and as soon as we identified ourselves with our badges and credentials, she shocked us by telling us that she knew exactly what we were there for, to hold on, and that she would be right back. A minute later she came back to the door with a small, insulated lunch box which she handed to us. We then asked if we could come in and look around to make sure there wasn't more money or drugs in the house. She answered okay and let us in. We searched the residence thoroughly and then left with the $30,000. We then went back to the office to start seizure proceedings for the seized currency.

Here is the tragic part. About two months after this, Fitz went out to get a pizza for dinner. She had left her young daughter at her home with her mother. When she got home, just as she got to the front door of the house, and right in front of both her daughter and mother who had heard her and met her at the door, someone from behind the bushes alongside the front door stepped out, put a gun to the back of Fitz's head, and pulled the trigger. She died in front of her daughter and mother.

It broke my heart to hear this as this was my investigation, and we were the ones who had seized the money. Don't get me wrong. What we did was perfectly legal and it was just good dope cop work. But these things happened in the circles that we ran in. I have always said it's the children, and wives, and mothers, and fathers of these drug dealers who got destroyed by these parasites.

To me, there was no doubt what had happened. Unfortunately, we couldn't prove it as there were no eyewitnesses. And all of our other leads didn't pan out. It still haunts me to this day. And that was my introduction to Robbie Long.

Back to the SNP investigation! One decision that had to be made was which sub-group of the SNP should be tackled first as the SNP had two sub-groups. They had the drug trafficking group which provided a steady stream of cash for the organization, and then there was the Homicide Squad or The Cut-Throat Committee. They were the enforcers of the gang, as I previously mentioned. They protected their members from rival gangs, but they also specialized in home invasions. They would hear by word of mouth, or rumors on the street, that a rival organization or drug dealer had received a large quantity of drugs. They would then stalk these other members, determine where they lived and then soon after, in the middle of the night, force their way in with guns blazing. They would shoot and kill whoever got in the way and would leave with the stash of drugs and whatever other contraband could be found. They were modern day pirates. Subsequently, we decided to go after the drug trafficking group first.

Now that we had an objective, we had to figure a way to get us there. We tried to think of the normal investigative techniques to take down this organization. We could try to recruit informants. We could try to put witnesses in front of the Grand Jury. We could rely on surveillance alone. We could conduct controlled buys of drugs using undercover agents. I could go on and on. It was then decided that none of these techniques could be used alone effectively. What we needed to do was apply a number of them at the same time **in conjunction** with a wiretap investigation.

I was in heaven. This was my wheelhouse. This is what I had done for years. Knowing about my past and wiretap successes, I was chosen to be the affiant. I couldn't wait to get started. And the best way to dirty someone's cell phone was to have them use it to complete drug transactions. While I was busy formulating an outline for the affidavit and doing my research, the rest of the team was conducting surveillance on various members of the organization while also trying to recruit an informant that could purchase drugs from one of the SNP members. One day, we got a break.

A female who had been arrested and wanted to cooperate with law enforcement in hopes of leniency, mentioned during her post-arrest interview that she knew a Jermonte Fletcher. Fletcher, who also went by "Chin" or "Beans," was a member of the SNP. When asked if she knew his cell phone number, she replied that she didn't at the time, but she was sure that she could ask around and get it, and she eventually did. She was then asked if she would be willing to call Fletcher to see if he would sell her crack cocaine, her drug of choice. She replied that she didn't see why not since she had purchased drugs in the past from him. And that's what she did.

As I was busy writing the affidavit and completing the Organized Crime Drug Enforcement Task Force (OCDETF) proposal, which was required for funding, the rest of the team was using this female to make several controlled buys from Fletcher. Every contact that she made with Fletcher was recorded. After every buy, the detectives controlling the female would transcribe the calls and get them to me. I would then add them to the affidavit. It was a slow and tedious process, but it was getting closer to completion with each passing day.

We then had to think of an operation name. Every major investigation like this had an operational name. So, we tried to think of what we could come up with using some sort of tie in with Short North Posse. We believed that the name should somehow tie in with the investigation. For example, when I was in Miami in 1992, we had an investigation with ties to Toronto. The Toronto Blue Jays had just won the World Series that year, so we titled the operation, Operation Blue Jay. Now what could we do with Short North Posse? We wanted to stay away from "posse" since that had some sensitive undertones. And the word "north" is so common. We tried to focus on the word "short." And somehow it just popped in my head. I had remembered a movie that was pretty popular in its day called *Get Shorty*. Not only did it have a reference to the word "short," but also the word "get" to me was a perfect tie-in to "Let's get them," or "Let's take them down." The rest of the team overwhelmingly approved, and it was then referred to as "Operation Get Shorty."

After months of work and numerous controlled buys, the affidavit was eventually completed and we were ready to send it off to DOJ/Main Justice for review. After that it would then go to a federal judge for final approval. This part of the Title III wiretap process was always trying to me since the attorney reviewer at DOJ/Main Justice reviewed the affidavit with a fine-tooth comb. Then they sent it back with their comments and corrections. Those corrections and edits were made and then it went back to DOJ/Main Justice. This back and forth went on for a week or two until it was finally approved. Then it took a day or two to get the Attorney General's (AG's) approval. At that point, his or her signature was just a rubber stamp, but it still took a day or two since the AG was so busy. Once completed, a federal judge in the district, in this case the Southern District of Ohio (SDOH), signed it. After that we were off to the races.

This wiretap was no different than any other except that there was a lot of gang lingo that I had to familiarize myself with. Yes, there was the normal drug lingo that I knew from doing years of dope work, but terms like 'strap,' 'gat,' and 'heater' were all new to me. A strap is code word for a gun since sometimes it was strapped to your body in a holster. A gat is short for a Gatling gun. And a heater is another slang term for a gun because when it's fired, it's like a mini-explosion and the barrel of the gun gets very hot. The shell casings are also extremely hot. So, a heater.

We started slowly by just listening for the first week or so. It was important to just listen at first to get to know the members of the organization and associates and their voices, as well as residences, stash houses, and drug holes. After that, we then increased surveillance on Fletcher and his close circle. After getting to know the players and identifying all of the locations frequented by the organization, the next big step in any wiretap was to validate the wire.

The last thing we wanted to do was arrest everyone involved in the organization on conversations alone. It could be done but it was not easy. It was called a dry conspiracy. Validating a wire was listening to a conversation on the wire about a planned drug transaction, and then making a traffic stop based on probable cause and seizing the drugs.

Anyway, we were successful with making a few drug seizures in our investigation including this crazy one. The next part of this story took us to Logan, West Virginia. Whenever the line went quiet, it was never a good thing. Usually, it meant that the targets were tipped off about their phones being tapped, and they dropped it to go buy another. In this case, our line had been quiet for a few days. We had no idea what was going on. We were scratching our heads and trying to figure it out. We had been really careful on surveillance, so we didn't think that surveillance was the reason. And we hadn't arrested anyone, so it couldn't be because of that and the ensuing discovery process. We had yet to make a traffic stop to validate the wire which was always risky. We had no idea. And then, just as quickly as it went dead, the line came back to life and there was Fletcher making phone calls. We had just about given up on the line and were about to shut the investigation down, or at least try to find Fletcher's new phone.

What had happened was that Fletcher had gone down to Logan, West Virginia. We didn't know this at first but were able to piece together enough intelligence information that led us to Logan, West Virginia. He had gone down there to set up a drug network in that part of the state. And who knows why he picked Logan! If you've ever been to Logan, you would know why I said that. Fletcher had returned and was bragging about what a sweet set-up he had down there, that it was out in the middle of nowhere, and that he already had a bunch of customers. He went on and on and on. Whew! Well, at least our wiretap was still up and running.

I contacted the office in Charleston, West Virginia which covered Logan. It just so happened that one of the TFOs with the Charleston office was a local officer for the Logan Police Department. For that reason, he was the one that was assigned to assist us.

When I finally called this officer, I told him what we had going with Fletcher and what our investigation was all about. I then went on to tell him about Fletcher's recent trip down to Logan to set up a local drug ring. I was hoping that he could use an informant, or local intelligence information or something to identify the individuals involved in this new drug ring. I mean, if there was a black guy from Columbus going to a town like Logan, which was predominantly white, to set up a drug ring, it was probably not going to go unnoticed for long. The second point of my phone call was about asking for assistance with surveillance if and when Fletcher returned to Logan. He responded that he would be glad to help. That was all I could ask for at that point.

Well, it didn't take long for Fletcher to get this new drug ring in Logan up and running and in business. One day we picked up a call on the wire. I remember it being weird because after all this time on the wiretap, we recognized most of the names and voices. This call was between Fletcher and a guy with a real thick Southern accent. This had to be the Logan connection!

The individual asked Fletcher if could sell him eight of the "hard." The code word "hard" was easy. Hard has always been street slang for crack cocaine since it was cooked from powder cocaine into rock cocaine. But that didn't make sense either since Fletcher was mostly a weed and pill dealer. He didn't usually mess with cocaine, crack cocaine or heroin for the most part, especially that large of an amount. Sure, he sold crack cocaine to our informant to start the wiretap investigation but that was only a few grams each buy.

So, we were a little stumped there. And the code word "eight" could be in reference to grams or ounces or even an "eight ball" which is slang for an eighth of an ounce which is approximately 3.5 grams. We just didn't know at that point. What we did know, however, and all agreed that we were going to have to go after this one and try to make a traffic stop. Not only was the wiretap coming to an end (we had been up for almost two months at that point), but it was crack cocaine which carries with it a much stiffer penalty than marijuana or prescription pills. **We were going to validate the wire!**

We quickly put together a surveillance team that established itself in the vicinity of Fletcher's apartment. The plan would be to wait for the target – he went by Bobby – to arrive at Fletcher's to pick up the crack. We would then follow the vehicle and make a traffic stop based on probable cause. So, all we could do for the moment was to wait and key off of the phone calls coming into

Fletcher. Simple, right? Not even close. About four hours later, we intercepted a call. It was Bobby telling Fletcher that he was almost there and if he was ready. Logan was about three and a half hours south of Columbus, so the timing was about right. Fletcher stated that he was. Surveillance eventually picked up on an unfamiliar car arriving at the parking lot adjacent to Fletcher's apartment. Bobby had arrived. He was with another individual who we learned later was Bobby's friend. His name was Doug. Bobby and Doug. Bobby left the vehicle while Doug stayed in the car. Bobby was only in the apartment for a few minutes and then he left. Surveillance observed Bobby exit the apartment, enter his vehicle, and depart from the area. And it was on. Surveillance on Bobby and Doug ensued for about 15 minutes. The surveillance stopped when Bobby and Doug arrived at a different apartment complex in a different section of Columbus. We had no idea what was going on, but it got extremely frustrating really fast.

What we didn't realize, but made sense afterwards, was that Fletcher had simply brokered the deal. He was a middleman. As I stated earlier, Fletcher was a weed and prescription pill dealer, not a crack dealer. But he wanted Bobby and Doug's business, of course. Fletcher wasn't going to turn down something this easy for some good old hard cash. We found out later that all Fletcher did was to put Bobby and Doug in touch with an associate of his in Columbus who cooked crack.

When Bobby and Doug had showed up at Fletcher's, it was simply to pay Fletcher for the crack cocaine. Fletcher then sent Bobby and Doug over to the associate's apartment to wait while the crack was being cooked. Fletcher told Bobby and Doug that he would pay the associate out of the money that Bobby and Doug had just given him minus a "cut" for himself as his broker or middleman fee. So, that's why Bobby and Doug led surveillance to that other apartment. And here was where it got frustrating. After waiting for four hours for Bobby and Doug to drive to Columbus, they were now just sitting outside of this random apartment waiting for the crack to cook. And this went on for hours. Once in a while Bobby would call Fletcher asking what was taking so long. In turn, Fletcher would call his associate, get the update, and then call Bobby back with the update. It was tedious and tiring.

You might be wondering why Fletcher just didn't put Bobby in touch with his associate directly. Drug dealers never did this. They protected their assets as Fletcher's role in this was a broker or middleman. He was getting a cut of the profits. If he were to introduce his associate to Bobby, then Bobby wouldn't need Fletcher anymore. The associate needed Fletcher to bring him customers. Bobby and Doug needed Fletcher since he had the connection for crack cocaine. If Fletcher took himself out of this relationship, he wouldn't be needed anymore and subsequently, wouldn't be paid.

Everyone has a role in the drug trafficking trade. It's all compartmentalized and it's meant that way for a reason. DTOs do this to protect themselves and insulate themselves. Everyone has a role but that's all they know and they don't know anyone else in the organization. That way, if a member gets stopped by law enforcement he or she can't cooperate and "rat" on someone else. The collateral damage is minimal because *they don't know anything.*

Finally, after waiting for hours, the wire room picked up a call in which Fletcher told Bobby that the crack cocaine was ready and that someone would be out to his car shortly. Sure enough, surveillance units observed an individual walk out to Bobby and Doug's car and give them what appeared to be a folded paper towel. We could only assume that the crack cocaine was hidden inside. Surveillance then watched as Bobby and Doug departed the area not knowing that they were being followed. It was just past midnight.

We had to be careful with surveillance for a number of reasons. First, since the car driven by Bobby had just shown up, we were unable to install a tracker on the car. Additionally, we did not have any kind of tracking device on the cell phone being used by Bobby. In law enforcement there is a way to have the cell phone provider for a particular phone send you GPS locations as long as the phone was on. In law enforcement circles it was referred to as a "PING" order since we were basically pinging the cell tower and asking for the phone's location. It may seem complicated, but it was really not.

When powered up, every cell phone does the exact same thing. It constantly sends a message out to the cell tower through the network basically saying, "I'm on, I'm here," And that way, when an incoming phone call gets routed through the cell tower, it knows to send the call to your phone and not to voice mail. It does require a court order with a judge's signature, and we do need some probable cause, but they are relatively easy to obtain. However, just like the tracker and Bobby's car, the same held true for the PING order. We had just encountered Bobby for the first time that day, so we were unable to get a PING order for his phone.

You might be wondering why this helped on surveillance. When we had a PING order, we could ping the phone every minute, two minutes, five minutes, whatever time frame we wanted. We set the time interval. And then a geo location of that phone would be sent to whatever device we wanted – our computer, laptop, tablet, or cell phone. And this way, surveillance units just needed to ping the phone every couple of minutes to see its location. So, wherever the phone was, the car was too. It allowed surveillance units to follow from afar and eliminated the need to see the target car in order to follow it. You could actually be miles away and follow it.

The other reason we had to be careful was that it was past midnight. And our DEA aircraft could not be launched to assist with surveillance as normal since DEA pilots do not fly at night. The plane, which was always a huge advantage, could not be used. Every DEA division had an airwing which included at least one plane, depending on the size of the office, and at least two pilots to support DEA missions. It was an incredible advantage when following someone. The plane could fly thousands of feet in the air and follow the vehicle while transmitting the vehicle's location to the ground units by putting it out on the DEA radio. Additionally, each aircraft was fitted with a high tech, extremely powerful camera which could be used to zoom in on license plates, addresses, and even an individual's face. That was why there was always a spotter in the back. The spotter was another DEA agent who didn't mind flying and didn't get air sick easily. He basically assisted the pilot with the camera and the radio transmission to the ground units. That way, all the pilot had to do was fly the plane and focus on safety.

The third reason we had to be careful was that we were going to try to do a traffic stop using probable cause to affect the traffic stop. If Bobby and Doug observed surveillance or "made us," or "burned surveillance," two common terms law enforcement used to describe when the targeted individuals realize that they were being followed by law enforcement, a traffic stop that same day, or in this case that night, would seem awfully suspicious and coincidental. So, without a tracker, a PING order, or DEA Airwing at our disposal, we had to be extremely careful.

It also didn't help that we were driving through Southern Ohio and eventually crossing into West Virginia, an area **totally** unfamiliar to us. With all of those factors, we made a command decision to take the surveillance way out of Columbus before we would attempt to make the traffic stop, maybe all the way to Logan. Normally, we would wait a few minutes to affect the traffic stop but in order to protect the wire, we didn't want the traffic stop to lead back to Columbus or even Ohio. So, if the stop could be made far away from Columbus, Ohio in West Virginia, that would be even better. Anyway, a decision had been made. We settled in for a long night as we tried to keep our surveillance units back as far as possible while also keeping track of the red taillights of Bobby's vehicle flickering in the dark Ohio night.

As we attempted to follow Bobby and Doug, we observed some strange tactics. Bobby kept taking these crazy back roads, the kind that are windy and curvy with zero streetlights and are barely even paved. We weren't sure why and were worried that they had seen vehicles following them. Drug dealers who suspected that they were being followed often deployed these kinds of tactics to see if the car or cars behind them would also take the isolated side road. We just weren't sure. All we could do was pull over and wait to see if they made a U-turn and eventually come back out to the main highway.

We also waited a few minutes and then sent a surveillance unit down each sideroad they took, looking down the driveways of the houses on each road just in case they had pulled into a residence for some reason. We also pulled up maps of the area on our cell phones and sent surveillance units down parallel roads hoping to shadow them that way. And it worked. Well, it either worked or we got extremely lucky because we kept managing to find Bobby and Doug one way or another. It went like that throughout the night. What they were doing was most surprising.

As we got closer and closer to the area of Logan, I called the TFO in the Charleston office that I had spoken to previously and informed him of what was going on. I apologized for calling so late but I told him that I wanted to make sure that we were committed to heading towards Logan first. I didn't want to put out a false alarm and then have Bobby and Doug drive somewhere else. I wanted to be sure, as I explained to the TFO, and now I was pretty sure because Logan was only about 15 to 20 minutes away. He stated that he would gather some agents and TFOs from the office and have them post up in the area of the highway as it came into the Logan area. I thanked him greatly and we continued with our surveillance.

Then an incredibly funny thing happened. At one point, we had lost Bobby and Doug. We were so pissed. To come so far and to lose them was really frustrating. They had taken a few quick rights and lefts, and we were unable to keep up with them. We never did find out exactly where they went, but again, we kept running into them and resuming surveillance. Who knows? Maybe they had stopped for gas, or a quick trip through a drive through, but somehow, we kept finding them.

It also helped that by this time, we were actually in Logan and it was in the middle of the night, so there weren't too many cars on the road at that point. Just us and Bobby and Doug! Then we lost them

188 – CHAPTER 30 - SHORT NORTH POSSE (SNP)

again! I remember pulling off to the side of the road hoping that someone would put out on radio traffic that they had found Bobby and Doug. I mean, there was no sense driving when we had no idea where the target was and nowhere to go at the moment. Afterall, Bobby and Doug could have been driving in the exact opposite direction. I was so frustrated that it only made sense to pull over and wait. A few minutes later, the radio crackled, and someone put out on the radio that they had found Bobby and Doug's vehicle.

As soon as they put out the location, and I figured which way I needed to go, I stormed off easily breaking the speed limit by a huge margin. Sure enough, in the pitch-black night I saw blue lights in my rear-view mirror. **Shit!** I was going to get stopped. And within a second, I had a West Virginia State Trooper at my window asking for my license and registration. It was a very nice female trooper and as she reached my window I quickly apologized, showed her my badge and credentials, and explained why I was going so fast. She quickly told me to get going and wished me luck. So, I stormed off again. Just as I had reached the area where the agent or TFO had seen Bobby and Doug, another radio transmission came out saying that they had lost them again. **Damn!** So close!

You might be thinking that we didn't have a very good surveillance team. But we did. Very good. It was just extremely challenging to follow their car undetected on a deserted highway in the middle of the night and in a town with no cars around that could that we could blend in with. There were also no cars on the roads. So, I pulled over again and waited. Same routine. We all posted up around different parts of Logan and waited. Sure enough, a radio transmission came out from an agent or TFO saying that they had found the car driven by Bobby and Doug. I roared off again in hot pursuit.

Within a minute or two as I was getting closer and closer to where Bobby and Doug had been spotted, I saw blue lights behind me again. What? *This can't be happening to me again!* As the officer, a West Virginia State Trooper again, started walking toward my vehicle, I realized that **it was the same** female trooper. As she got to my window and saw me smiling, she screamed out over and over, "Oh my God, oh my God, get going, get going, I am **so** sorry!!" That was the first time in my 29-year career that I was stopped by the same officer on two separate occasions in the same night in the same investigation in the same small town. I'll always remember that.

We were actually able to maintain surveillance on Bobby and Doug the rest of the night. As surveillance progressed, I decided that it was time to turn the surveillance over to the agents and TFOs that had been set up in the Logan area since it was their back yard and they were familiar with the town. One by one, we peeled off as the crew from Logan took over surveillance. Eventually, a traffic stop was made based on probable cause. And, low and behold, Bobby had eight ounces of crack cocaine in his front pocket! **Boom!** Bobby and Doug were then both arrested and transported back to the local Sheriff's office for booking and processing. This was where it all went bad and downhill.

No one was to blame. No one did anything malicious or on purpose. It was just some careless behavior. While Bobby and Doug were back at the sheriff's office being booked and processed, the agents and TFOs that had assisted us that night were in the next room whooping it up and celebrating and giving each other high fives. You see, eight ounces of crack cocaine was a **lot** anywhere, but in Logan it was a **huge** seizure. They were just excited and celebrating which I got, and I had no problem with. Maybe next time, though, they should do it at a bar down the street or after Bobby and Doug had been processed and booked and transported to the county jail.

What happened was that during this celebration, one of the agents or TFOs asked how this all started. And someone said in reply, "It came from a wiretap in Columbus." Bobby and Doug, sitting there in the next room heard it all. At this point, no one realized that Bobby and Doug had heard this. It wasn't until the next day when Bobby was allowed to make his first phone call from jail and decided to call Fletcher. We sat in horror in the wire room listening with a pit in our stomachs as Bobby explained to Fletcher in great detail what he had heard the night before through the wall. And the wiretap ended with Bobby stating, "Bro, your phone is tapped. They're listening to everything you say." And that was it. Over. The wiretap was done as Fletcher immediately stopped using that phone. As my grandfather always used to say, when something was over, "Good-Bye, Charlie."

Just a quick side note. We eventually interviewed both Bobby and Doug down the road after they had been arrested and when both had decided to cooperate and plead guilty. After the first interview where they both told us all of the details about picking up the crack cocaine from Fletcher, we just had to ask. We wanted to know what the hell they were doing that night taking all of those crazy-ass side roads and dirt roads. Are you ready for this? They were looking for a deer to kill. We were like, "Huh?" Bobby explained that they were both big deer hunters, but that Doug had never killed a deer. So, Bobby said that he was determined to find a deer for Doug to kill. And this was with eight ounces of crack cocaine in his pocket! And here we were thinking that they had burned surveillance, but it was simply two jackasses hunting deer in the middle of the West Virginia night!

It was fine with me. Wiretap investigations were brutal, especially on our families. We worked almost around the clock and between writing affidavits, affidavit extensions, ten-day reports for the judge, wire room shifts and surveillance shifts, there was not much time for anything else in our lives. So, I was ready. Besides, we had identified almost everyone in Fletcher's organization over the past two months, and we had made a really nice eight-ounce crack cocaine seizure. It was time. But the investigation was far from over.

The next step was to decide if we were going to present the case to a sitting federal grand jury, or if we were going to write a criminal complaint. There was a big difference. Basically, if we wanted to present the case to a federal grand jury, we had to present government witnesses to the grand jury who, under oath, would provide testimony to the grand jury members under the direction of the prosecutor. And we'd continue to present these witnesses to the grand jury on a once-a-week basis until our case was presented. Then the grand jury members had to decide if they wanted to issue a "true bill" which was legal-ease for determining if there was enough probable cause to issue arrest warrants.

If we would have taken the route of a criminal complaint, that would have involved writing a lengthy affidavit which would have been presented to a Magistrate Judge who would then determine if the probable cause presented in the affidavit met the threshold to issue arrest warrants. We took the route of the grand jury since it was much easier to shuttle witnesses before the grand jury on a week-to-week basis, one at a time, to provide testimony, then writing a massive, lengthy affidavit. So, that's what we did.

In December 2013, the testimony before the grand jury was complete and the grand jury issued a true bill.

A press release on December 11, 2013 from both DOJ and the SDOH, stated that 22 individuals had been charged in a drug trafficking investigation that lasted for approximately one year. The release stated that the organization was based in the Columbus area and had been investigated by the FBI, the DEA, the Franklin County Sheriff's Office, the Columbus Police Department, the Bureau of Alcohol, Tobacco and Firearms (ATF), and the Franklin County Prosecutor's Office. This investigation resulted in an indictment that included 78 separate counts. In addition to drug trafficking, the counts also involved conspiracy and weapon charges.

Specifically, the indictment charged that the organization trafficked in cocaine, crack cocaine, marijuana, and prescription drugs, specifically oxycodone. The defendants in this organization could receive between 10 years and life for these offenses. Additionally, the press release went on to state that the indictment charged the defendants with possession of a weapon while conducting a drug trafficking crime, as well as possession of a weapon by a convicted felon and traveling across state lines to conduct drug trafficking activities and money laundering.

192 – *CHAPTER 30 - SHORT NORTH POSSE (SNP)*

The press release went on to commend AUSA Dave DeVillers and AUSA Kevin Kelley, the two principal federal prosecutors in the investigation.[2]

What happened next was a bit of a mystery to me. I never really understood it. In all of my years of law enforcement, once the drug trafficking organization was indicted and the arrest warrants issued, the next step was to plan the raid, or take down. Normally, an extensive and detailed plan was drawn up using SWAT teams and agency Entry Teams to conduct pre-dawn raids and search warrants. The search warrants were executed and the individuals inside were arrested. It was pretty simple. The two went hand in hand because then you were totally covered. You had the legal right to enter the residence and then the legal right to arrest the individual as well.

In this case, a decision was made to conduct a search warrant at the residence of Fletcher but not arrest him at the time. It was thought that if he was given a chance to talk and cooperate, we might gain more insight to the investigation, as well as the SNP organization, and maybe Fletcher would be willing to give up his source of supply for his narcotics (the only member of the DTO that we were never able to identify), or some intelligence information related to the Homicide Squad or Cut-Throat Committee members. The problem with this thinking was that when someone was looking at the amount of prison time that Fletcher was facing, he usually wouldn't give you that kind of information unless he had silver bracelets on while he was getting carted off to jail to face a 20-year sentence. It just was not happening. We had to have something to hold over their heads.

The day of reckoning came. We seized some cash, drugs, and guns. The usual but not any less important. Fletcher was interviewed and questioned. He gave very limited information, a lot of "I don't know his name," and "I only know his street name – Snots," or "I have no idea where he lives." Some other answers were "I used to have his cell, but he changed it," or "I haven't seen him in weeks," and "I think he's out of the dope game." Typical. At the end of the day, we left. And Fletcher was allowed to go. I remember being so frustrated by this. The team tried to reassure me that he would be arrested eventually but that they wanted to give him another chance to cooperate.

Guess what happened? He fled! He ran and was eventually declared a DEA fugitive. He was a fugitive for over a year.

When an arrest warrant is issued for an individual, DEA policy dictated that we had ten days to apprehend him or her before the individual was declared a fugitive. The DEA delegated the fugitive apprehension to the U.S. Marshal's Service. After Fletcher was declared a fugitive, the U.S. Marshal's Fugitive Task Force received the investigation. However, I continued to work it and search for Fletcher on my own when time allowed. I wasn't about to give up on him after all of that hard work we all had put in.

I tried to find him the best that I could. At one point, I completed numerous cell phone searches in which I sent subpoenas containing Fletcher's most frequently called numbers, say seven or eight of them, to every major cell phone carrier. I requested that these companies query their systems and give me whatever cell phone numbers, hopefully one or two of the same local numbers, that had in turn been calling those same numbers recently in hopes that the person would be Fletcher. After completing this subpoena and waiting for a couple of weeks while the cell phone companies did their workup, we finally received two possible numbers for Fletcher. I immediately went to the US Attorney's Office and completed a PING order to try to find the locations of the phones. This did not amount to anything as Fletcher had either used these phones and dumped them, or they were never in use by Fletcher to begin with. Unfortunately, this was not an exact science.

Of course, there were the normal jail house rats willing to tell you anything so that they could get out of prison, or at least have some prison time shaved off. Anytime I would hear that someone wanted to see me because he knew where Fletcher was, I would make an appointment with the Franklin County Jail and proceed to meet with the prisoner. Then he would tell me that a friend of a friend of a friend had seen Fletcher hanging out on the East Side. Then another said the same, but Fletcher was holed up on the South Side of Columbus. It was maddening. Of course, every time I would get a tip, I would spend hours in my car on surveillance just waiting to get a glimpse of Fletcher. But it wasn't to be. I wasn't surprised as these kinds of tips were usually a waste of time and resources. But I never knew when that one good tip might roll in. So, I treated them all as if they were the real deal. We even had Fletcher's photograph put up on one of those huge billboards on the South side of Columbus advertising a reward if any information given led to his arrest. That didn't work either.

I kept in touch with the U.S. Marshal's Service Fugitive Task Force this entire time, sharing information and leads with them. They would occasionally help me out on surveillance, and I did the same for them. But to no avail. Then, one day as I was driving to work, I received a call from the lead agent with the U.S. Marshal's Service Fugitive Task Force. I remember exactly what he said to me, "Hey, Keith, are you sitting down?" I laughed and said that I certainly hoped so since I was driving. And then I heard the words that I thought I would never hear and still shake me to this day. It wasn't the normal information that Fletcher had been arrested but that Fletcher had been killed!! I was not expecting that!

I almost jumped through the phone blurting out question after questions like "Wait, what?" and, "When, how?" When I finally gave the agent a moment to talk, he explained that late the night before, they had received a tip that Fletcher was staying with some old girlfriend on the South Side. He stated that they went out on surveillance at this apartment complex immediately and eventually observed Fletcher taking trash out to the dumpster later that same night. He apologized for not having informed me sooner, but he said that he lost track of everything. I understood as I knew it wasn't intentional and that I had been in that same position many times before.

The agent said it was pretty cut and dry. They knocked and announced their presence just like they always do and stated that they were federal agents. A female answered the door and appeared nervous and distraught. All of the sudden, Fletcher was moving down the stairs from the second-floor firing at the agents! He just wasn't going to be taken alive. Of course, the Fugitive Task Force returned fire killing Fletcher. By some miracle, not one single member of the Fugitive Task Force had been hit with any bullets fired by Fletcher! I couldn't believe it. Fletcher had once made statements that he was never returning to jail and he meant it. That was the end of the Jermonte Fletcher investigation. You live by the sword; you die by the sword.

Although that was the end of the Fletcher investigation, we had always planned to run this investigation in phases. As I mentioned earlier, the first phase was the drug trafficking organization phase, headed by Fletcher. And the other was the Homicide Squad or Cut-Throat Committee investigation. We launched that as soon as the dust had settled and all of the proffers, hearings and sentencings were completed in the Fletcher investigation.

This new phase was a much different type of investigation, one that centered mostly on grand jury testimony. We went out and found witness after witness who either knew these members or had worked with them in the past as co-conspirators or some that had been jilted or screwed and simply wanted revenge. We interviewed regular people, prisoners looking for some leniency, and other law enforcement officers, and even private investigators who had knowledge of one or more of the members. It was quite an experience to listen to these witnesses talk about how they would set up rival drug dealers and then conduct home invasions stealing the trafficker's drugs, money, and guns. And, if they resisted......well, they didn't get the name Homicide Squad or Cut-Throat Committee for nothing. These guys were stone cold killers. Some had five bodies on them (murders).

Well, we eventually indicted 20 members of the Homicide Squad or Cut-Throat Committee all on numerous counts. Thirteen of them pled guilty, six went to trial and one died in prison awaiting trial. In summary, we were able to obtain 31 murder-related convictions connected to 14 murders. At the time, it was the largest murder investigation in the history of the state of Ohio.

*****

The following is a summary of an interesting article about the Short North Posses (SNP).

According to the article, the SNP was the most well-known and notorious gang that had been known to the Columbus area. It mentioned that the gang had been around for over 25 years and has always had the reputation of being the most violent and the most aggressive around Columbus. Some residents claimed that the gang got a bad name and that, in the beginning, all they were trying to do was to protect the neighborhood. However, it was hard to defend the SNP when they turned to murder to protect their turf. The article then went on to say that perhaps the tide was turning after the dismantling of the SNP took place which was the direct result of a two-year investigation by the FBI, DEA, ATF, Columbus Police Department, and the Franklin County Sheriff's Office. This resulted in the indictment of 20 SNP members. AUSA Dave DeVillers stated that it was the largest murder investigation in Ohio history at the time of its completion. Even with this two-year investigation completed, others were skeptical. They cite the fact that on three other occasion – 1995, 2006 and 2010 – crackdowns on the SNP were made without the gang disappearing. They always seemed to be able to grow their head back, kind of like a snake.

Many local business and companies invested in the area and the Weinland Park Collaborative was formed in 2010. The number of interested businesses and companies has reached more than two dozen which has resulted in approximately $14 million being invested in the neighborhood. An additional $37 million in taxpayer money has also been infused into that area. Many agree that this has made a huge difference in the area and that it has vastly improved in the past two years. However, it all comes down to safety and security. Only the future can tell.

The following is a brief history of the SNP and its encounters with law enforcement:

- 1995: 46 SNP Members were indicted on 200 plus felony narcotics and gun charges.
- 1999: The U.S. Sixth Circuit Court of Appeals reversed conspiracy convictions and reduced the sentences of seven key members of the SNP who were charged in 1995.
- 2010: 19 members of the SNP were indicted by a Franklin County grand jury on numerous narcotics and gun charges.
- 2013: 22 members of the NSP were indicted by a Federal Grand Jury on drug trafficking, conspiracy, and weapon charges.
- 2014: 20 members of the SNP Homicide Squad/Cut-Throat Committee were arrested on federal murder charges.[3]

I have one last story about the SNP investigation that I'd like to add before I finish with the SNP. Long-term investigations were tough. They were sometimes very tedious with long hours, mundane activities, and periods of great boredom. The hours I have spent in my OGV staring at a house waiting for someone to come out the front door, or staring at a car waiting for it to move, were just too many to count. But the reward was often the key to any investigation. It was like the puzzle concept I mentioned previously in this book. That person coming out the front door or leaving in a car could sometimes be the last piece to the puzzle or at least a key piece.

This happened in the second phase of the SNP investigation when we turned our focus to the Homicide Squad or Cut-Throat Committee. We were investigating one of the home invasions that I spoke about earlier. But this was a bad one as it resulted in a murder. And it involved, who else, but Robbie Long, among others. When we investigated this particular home invasion, some of the cooperating defendants that we used told us that the group of home invaders used a silver-colored rental car to drive to and from the house that they had invaded. So, it meant only one thing. We had to find that rental car record. What a great piece of evidence that would be!!

Around the same time, we also learned that the local police department had responded to this home invasion. Obviously, we interviewed the two officers that responded to the residence that fateful evening. We wanted to know about any evidence that they had obtained that night and if there were any witnesses to the home invasion. During this interview, one of the patrol officers happened to mention that they had their dashboard camera operating as they drove to the scene in case one of the vehicles that was driving in the opposite direction could possibly turn out to be the fleeing suspects in the getaway car. He stated it was a long shot but that they always did that just in case they got lucky, and a witness might say that the perpetrators left in a red car, for example. Of course, this is not an exact science as the home invaders could have left in the completely opposite direction that night. But we stated that we still wanted to view it.

They eventually provided the video clip to us and, low and behold, we actually spotted a silver-colored vehicle pass the police cruiser going in the opposite direction. And when we slowed the tape down, we could see that the vehicle was occupied by four individuals, the exact number of home invaders whom the cooperating defendants told us that night. Could that possibly be the vehicle? Maybe. It was just a piece of the puzzle.

The next step was to go the local rental car company and find that record. Hopefully, it would be in one of the home invader's names and would have the color of the vehicle listed as silver. We contacted the local rental car company and to our amazement they stated that they did not keep computer records going that far back. Unreal. I mean, this was 2014! We then asked if we could send a subpoena to their headquarters. The woman on the phone stated that we could but without a record locator number, it would be unsuccessful. We then asked if they could just search by a name and the lady stated that they didn't organize their database like that. Although very frustrated at that point, I remember asking if they kept any paper copies of the rental agreements anywhere. I was happy to hear that they did. The lady from the rental car company then gave me the address of a warehouse where we could go to search for the record. I had been hoping that she could've just gone into the back room of their office that day and within a minute or two come out with a rental car record. No such luck.

The next day we grabbed a couple of other FBI agents and proceeded to the warehouse. When we got there, we were greeted by one of the warehouse workers and taken to the back of the warehouse. Once there, we were shown boxes, literally **hundreds** of boxes, just heaped in a huge pile. It was a mess. I recall thinking that there was no way we were going to find this record. Absolutely no way.

To add to our frustration, it was summer in Ohio, and it was hot as hell and as with most warehouses, there wasn't any air conditioning! But we had no choice. We had to give it a go and do the best we could. We started going through boxes, one at a time. It took hours and hours. Basically, the entire day. The boxes weren't organized with markings or labels so we just had to grab a box, one by one, and go through it looking for one of the home invader's names (by that time we knew the identities of all four of the home invaders). The only thing that helped us was the fact that we knew the month and year, obviously, of the home invasion. So, if we started looking through a box and saw that the year of the rental was anything but 2014, we just moved on to another box. Then it happened. I found it!

At the end of the day and dripping in sweat, I found a rental car agreement in the name of Robbie Long. However, my utter shock and surprise in finding it was quickly met with confusion. The rental car agreement was for a vehicle that was not silver in color and it was for the time period starting the day **after** the home invasion. We were so confused by this. Why would Long rent a car the day after? But at least we had a rental record locator that we could use in an attempt to get more information and shed some light on the situation.

The very next day I called the rental car company's headquarters instead of the local branch hoping for some better luck than we got a few days before. And, man oh man, did we! Jackpot! The lady on the phone was incredibly helpful. She proceeded to take the record locator number and run it in their system. Then, and this is rare, but it does happen, she stated that she would give me the information over the phone and then send me a copy if I promised to send her a subpoena after the fact. Normally, the business, or whoever you are issuing the subpoena to, require the subpoena up front before issuing any information or documents. You can't blame them as there could be legal issues down the road for the business or entity if they don't have a subpoena on hand to back them up. Anyway, I promised her that I would do it as soon as I hung up the phone. And I did, for the record. And then I was blown away.

The woman on the phone proceeded to tell me that there was another rental car agreement associated with this record locator number. She said that since it was a continuation of the rental period, they used the same record locator number. Now I was really confused. However, she cleared things up for me quickly. As she read me the information over the phone, I remember being speechless and just sitting there with my mouth open. Long had rented a SILVER vehicle the day before the home invasion. It was in his name. He returned the vehicle the day after the home invasion and requested a new vehicle that he was due to return the following day. The comments section of the rental car agreement stated that Long didn't like the way the car was running. So, he returned that vehicle (the silver one) and rented another one for the rest of the time period. That was the rental car agreement that I had found in the warehouse.

But here's the real kicker. Further down in the comments section, the person who processed the return of the silver rental car at the facility – the person responsible for cleaning it, washing it, and making sure the gas had been filled – noted that the car was a mess and that it looked like there was ketchup spilled on the seats. **That was blood!** There was no doubt in my mind. Of course, how was the poor guy at the rental car company supposed to know that? He cleans the car and puts it back in space A14 or whatever. He's not expecting to see blood in the car.

Could it have been ketchup? Sure, I guess. But it was all over the back seats, not just a blob that a child could have dropped from a ketchup packet while eating French fries. Plus, we knew from the cooperating defendants that the murder victim that night didn't go quietly as he struggled and fought the home invaders the entire time until he ceased. So, I'm sure that the home invaders' clothes were covered in blood. Additionally, we also knew from the cooperating defendants that the modus operandi of these home invasion crews was to always bring a change of clothes with them. They did this for two reasons. One was to change their appearance in case a witness gave a description of their clothes to the police. The other was that if they were stopped by the police driving away or seen by someone else, they wouldn't be seen with blood-stained clothes. I'm sure that being covered in blood during the drive from the residence that night, **plus** changing clothes in the car, clothes covered in blood, could easily resemble ketchup everywhere.

To be honest, it didn't matter. The blood in the back seat could never be proven in court. But we had Long in a silver rental car on the night of the home invasion. This was corroborated by the cooperating defendants and also observed by the police dashboard camera. It wasn't a slam dunk, but it was pretty damn close. And that was the final piece of the puzzle for Robbie Long.

As the investigation wound down and only the court proceeding, change of plea hearings, sentencings, and trials remained, I found myself involved in yet another wiretap investigation, the last one that I would do during my stint at the FBI. It was the Mike Edwards investigation. More on that in a minute. I have to tell you the final chapter as it concerns my involvement in the Short North Posse investigation. And it's quite funny.

As the not guilty pleas turned into guilty pleas and the defendants started receiving their sentences, the thought turned to a possible jury trial for those that had refused to plead guilty up to that point. That's their constitutional right. I had no problem with that, and as I mentioned in the beginning of this book, I'm a trial man. I loved trials. They didn't bother me at all although they brought with them a tremendous amount of work. I mean, we have witness preparation, evidence cataloguing and preparation of transcripts (wiretap investigations, especially, since the calls had to be transformed into a transcript that the jury could follow along). And those were just a few tasks associated with a trial. As we neared the point where we were going to pull all of the deals and pleas and everything else off the table, only a handful decided to go to trial. And one of those was my old friend, Robbie Long.

Before I continue, one interesting thing about this investigation was that since a lot of these defendants were facing the death penalty, the DOJ mandated, as they always do, that the defendants could hire any defense attorney they wanted, paid for by the DOJ, regardless of the price. In a normal criminal case, the defendants had the right to hire a private defense attorney, but they had to pay for that person and that defense. Otherwise, they had to utilize an attorney afforded to them by the Public Defenders' office for free. Long hired a very expensive defense attorney, one of the best in the city of Columbus. As a matter of fact, Long hired the exact same one that he told Karen Fitz to deliver the $30,000 to! Long was headed to trial and one of the primary witnesses that was scheduled to testify against him was me! Bring it! Mano a mano.

After being prepped for trial by AUSA Dave DeVillers and AUSA

Kevin Kelley, I soon learned that I would be testifying to the facts of the investigation in which I first met Long, the controlled delivery of the marijuana from Mexico to El Paso to Columbus. Basically, they wanted me to lay out for the jury that Long had been doing this for a long time and that his tenure with the SNP wasn't a one-time thing and that he had been involved in criminal activity, in this case, drug trafficking, for a long time. They basically wanted me to explain to the jury that Long was a career criminal.

The day of the trial eventually arrived, and I showed up at the courthouse in my suit ready to testify. It was no big deal as I had done it many times before. The only wildcard was, like always, the defense attorney's questioning on cross examination. We knew that they were going to try to rip us apart, discredit us, shoot holes through our case, anything they could do to turn one juror. Just one, as that's all they'd need. So, I got prepped again in the witness room by AUSA Kelley right before I took the stand. It was just a quick run-down of the facts of the case and the questions that he was going to ask me on the stand during direct examination. No problem.

Eventually they called my name. I walked in the courtroom and proceeded to get sworn in. I took a seat in the witness stand I went through direct examination led by AUSA Kelley. I proceeded to lay out the investigation, step by step, just as I did earlier in this book. No problems. Easy peasy. Now came the time for cross examination. I always got a little uptight at this point because, once again I had **no** idea what was coming at me. I couldn't believe it. **Softballs**. And I was pounding them out of the park. What I mean by softballs is easy questions. No brainers. Almost like the defense attorney never asked his client, Long, about the arrest at all. This guy was making a lot of money!!

The first question he asked me was if his client, Long, cooperated with us at the time of his arrest. At first, I thought this was some kind of a joke as if I was being set up. I remember thinking, *seriously?* But I remembered my old days of testifying when I was schooled at just answering the questions by Guy Lewis. I could hear his voice in the back of my head saying, "Don't play their games." And I did just that. I remember answering, "Um, no, not at all." And then I remember the defense attorney looking shocked and asking me why his client wasn't cooperative. And, I answered coolly, "Well, because he ran from us and we had to chase him until we were finally able to tackle him."

One of the recipients of the 2018 "Ohio Distinguished Law Enforcement Group Achievement Award" after completion of the SNP investigation.

The defense attorney, who looked so flustered and all out of sorts, then asked another question. He asked me if, after that one incident, if his client had been cooperative with us after that. Again, shaking my head I responded, "I'm sorry, but no." Looking even more flustered than before, the defense attorney asked me to explain. I mean, he was incredulous. I simply stated, "Well, when we had him in the booking room and were going through the normal booking and processing, he wouldn't even tell us his name. We had no idea who he was until the fingerprints came back from the FBI the following day. That isn't being very cooperative to me." And as soon as I said that, I heard someone in the jury chuckle quietly. They were actually enjoying this. And, at that point, I knew we had the jury.

They thought this was as ridiculous as I did. Just then the defense attorney yelled out, "No more questions, Your Honor." And that was it. Over. I mean a few more witnesses testified, but the nail was in the coffin. Long was found guilty.

I never understood it. That's all that defense attorney had for me? They were such ridiculous questions. Questions that I don't think he would have ever asked me if he knew the answers. And all that money that he was making. I didn't think he prepped Long at all, or he would have known the answers to those questions and would have never asked them. What a miscarriage of justice, in my opinion.

31
Mike Edwards Investigation

A s the Short North Posse investigation wound down and loose ends were being tied up, I was being pulled into another investigation. This one was also a wiretap investigation. I was still assigned to the FBI Safe Streets Task Force at that time with only about a year left of the three-year tour. We had received a tip from the FBI office down in the southern part of the state, in Portsmouth, Ohio. It involved a defense attorney by the name of John Defender operating down in their neck of the woods, but the part of the tip that involved the Columbus area was an individual by the name of Mike Edwards.

Edwards was a heroin and a pill trafficker who specialized in steroids. Edwards was a jacked-up "roid" head who lived on the west side of Columbus and had a large customer base there. He had strong ties to Defender and other individuals in the Portsmouth area, as well. As a matter of fact, Edwards employed Defender as his attorney of record. He had him on retainer. Edwards also provided heroin and again mostly steroids to customers in the Portsmouth area. Subsequently, after receiving the intelligence brief on both Defender and Edwards, the FBI office in Portsmouth wanted to know if we were interested. I definitely was and expressed interest immediately.

Not only did it mean that we were going to initiate another wiretap investigation, my forte, but I **hated** dirty attorneys. I had done an investigation into two dirty attorneys when I was assigned to the Providence office, so I had a taste of it back then. But that investigation didn't pan out the way I wanted it to. A rule among many attorneys, even prosecutors, was that they should never prosecute other attorneys, even if they were dirty, because it was career suicide. Many prosecutors, whether they were state or federal prosecutors, eventually went into private practice one day. And once the word was out that they prosecuted a fellow attorney, again no matter how dirty, they were black-balled from the industry. It was a creepy fraternity; band of brothers type of thing that I never understood.

There were dirty cops out there too, and although it wasn't a fun investigation by any means, I personally took afront to these people and would want those cops off the job immediately as they were a disgrace to the profession and a black eye to all of the good cops out there. I never understood that way of thinking although the prosecutors I worked with over the years were and still are some of my best friends. Sorry, I digress. Let's just say that the two attorneys that we went after at the time got off with a slap on the wrist. We'll just leave it at that. So, I wanted another crack at this attorney.

However, this was not going to be our typical wiretap investigation because it involved an attorney. And since Edwards had Defender on retainer, that meant that at any time there could be a call from Edwards to Defender or the opposite, Defender to Edwards. And this was going to pose a **huge** hurdle as there are certain constitutional rights or privileges that even Title 21 wiretap rules and regulations must honor like husband/wife privilege, doctor/patient privilege, **and** attorney/client privilege.

For those outside of law enforcement, it means that these conversations were privileged and could not be listened to **unless** there was evidence of a crime involved in these conversations. We could listen for a few seconds in the beginning of each conversation, but once it was determined that no illegal activity was being discussed, we **had** to turn the call off. We were allowed to spot check it every 30 seconds or so to see if they changed subjects and were now talking about criminal activity, but if they weren't, we had to turn off the conversation again. So, what we were going to do with the possibility of a phone call and conversation between Edwards and Defender was to employ a Taint Team.

A what? That was my response to the prosecutor at the very onset of the investigation when he learned that an attorney was involved. He informed us that a Taint Team had to be utilized. I had no idea what he was talking about at the time but soon discovered that a Taint Team was basically a separate team of agents and prosecutors that weren't connected with the investigation at all. Moreover, it was even better if the members of the Taint Team weren't even in the same unit to put even further distance between them and the actual investigators. And the purpose of a Taint Team was to be able to field and monitor any calls between Defender and Edwards. This way, we as the principal investigators wouldn't be able to hear them and possibly listen to privileged and confidential attorney/client discussions and "taint" the investigation. It made perfect sense, but it also placed a huge burden on the Taint Team individuals as they had their own jobs, their own investigations, and their own prosecutions, but it had to be done.

The wirerooms typically ran from 8:00 a.m. until 12:00 a.m. with two shifts. The first shift was 8:00 a.m. to 4:00 p.m. and second shift was 4:00 p.m. to 12:00 a.m. For each shift, normal investigators monitored the phone lines and then there was another agent or investigator completely detached from the investigation who sat in a corner and waited for that one call to come in between Defender and Edwards. If it did, we would see the number coming in, turn to the Taint Team members and tell them that it was Defender calling in, for example. They would then take a headset and plug it in to the wiretap machine so that no one else could hear it and proceed to listen to the call. If it was nothing privileged, we could play it back and listen to it. If it was privileged, the Taint Team member would have to record the call and deliver it the next day to the prosecutor that was assigned to the Taint Team. Then they would make the ultimate decision if the call was privileged or not. This only happened two or three times if my memory serves me right. And two out of the three were immediately deemed to not be privileged in which case we could listen to it. Only one call was thought to contain possible privileged conversation and thus had to be recorded and delivered to the Taint Team prosecutor. This prosecutor was not able to tell us the contents at the time.

We learned after the fact that this conversation had to do with Edwards spotting surveillance units following him during a recent surveillance. He proceeded to call Defender and ask him what to do. Defender responded that he should get rid of everything in the house immediately. We knew from all of our years of narcotics investigations and experience that Defender was telling Edwards to get rid of his heroin, steroids, and pills. More about this conversation later.

The investigation progressed as the weeks went on. We did a really good job of taking the information provided on the phone calls and then matching that information on the street to certain individuals, vehicles, and residences. We were expanding the organization almost daily which is always one of the goals of any wiretap investigation. We were even able to identify not only the source of supply for the heroin for Edwards, **but also** the source of supply for the drugs for that person. Because of that, we were able to expand our investigation two levels above Edwards, and that was huge.

Eventually we had hit a point in the investigation where we felt that we had identified everyone possible. I mean, we could always just keep going and going but federal judges frown on that as you would again be infringing on one of the most sacred rights in the U.S. and that's privacy of our communications with one another. Instead, we decided to take everything down and affect our early morning raids, arrest warrants, and search warrants. We did a pretty good job and arrested approximately 15 individuals including Edwards and his two sources of supply. We even seized about $150,000 U.S. currency from one of the sources of supply. Whatever happened to Defender? It's an interesting story.

We, as investigators, wanted him charged and arrested. The U.S. Attorney's Office did not support our view. We knew he was dirty and the one phone call between Edwards and Defender showed a clear obstruction of justice. It was obvious to us that Defender was telling Edwards to get rid of his heroin, steroids, and pills. But as much as we argued our side of the story, the answer didn't change and so it was no. This again goes back to what I said earlier in the book. Attorneys did not like to prosecute other attorneys, no matter which side that they were on. It was just one of those things. Call it a fraternity, or brotherhood, or a family, they just didn't like to prosecute one another no matter how dirty the bad attorney was. I never understood it and I never will. So, Defender walked.

There was only one time that I really had a sour taste in my mouth from this job. And that was the day I retired, June 30, 2020, knowing that Defender was still out there. I felt as if we hadn't finished the job. I felt as though I had let the public down by leaving this monster on the street. Then, just like a cool breeze on a hot summer day that catches you unexpectedly by surprise, a friend of mine alerted me to the existence of an article that spoke about Defender and his checkered past. And I was even mentioned in it!

To summarize, the article stated that the newspaper's investigation started after discovering an 80-page federal wiretap affidavit that had been written by Special Agent Keith Leighton, DEA Columbus, OH and filed in the SDOH in August of 2015. The affidavit documented the fact that Attorney John Defender had operated in the Portsmouth, Ohio area since the early 1970s. It went on to state that Defender had been linked to approximately 25 women whom Defender used for sexual favors in turn for judicial leniency and reduced legal fees.[4]

The women finally garnered the attention of federal law enforcement, mainly the FBI Portsmouth, Ohio office and the DEA Columbus, OH office, and proceeded to tell their stories to these agents. Defender was eventually charged and arrested on human trafficking and racketeering charges. Defender denied all wrongdoings.

One of the main reasons that Defender lasted for so long without justice, literally over 40 years, was that he thought that he was untouchable and above the law.

The modus operandi was always the same. The women almost all had the same story. They had been arrested for drug possession or drug trafficking. They would hire Defender for their attorney of record since Defender had the reputation of being able to obtain reduced jail sentences for his clients due to his close relationship with local law enforcement and the court system. However, part of the payment process was that the women had to agree to have sex with him as well as with his friends and associates. Ah, sweet justice.....finally!

32
Group Supervisor

After my three-year tour with the FBI had been completed, I returned to the DEA. I spent a year in the Tactical Diversion Squad, or TDS, which was a group of agents and TFOs that focused on the drug trafficking activities of doctors, pharmacists, and nurses. These groups strove to investigate, disrupt, and dismantle those in the medical field who were involved in the diversion of licit pharmaceutically controlled substances, or listed chemicals. It was interesting and definitely different, but it just wasn't my style. I was a street agent. Much of the time, the investigators in these groups stared at a computer screen all day and counted prescriptions. It was incredibly important because if we couldn't trust a doctor then who could we trust. It just wasn't for me.

Soon after that I was promoted to a Group Supervisor of a task force in the Columbus office. I had struggled my whole career with the decision to become a supervisor and enter the management ranks of the DEA. Early in my career, I wanted nothing to do with it. I wanted to be out there chasing bad guys and kicking down doors. I didn't want to sit behind a desk and push papers around. But I also thought that was a normal reaction of a 25-year-old right out of the academy.

When I hit about 25 years on with the DEA, my mind was in a different place. I first thought that slowing down a little bit would be good for me and the family. I was now 50 years old and too old to be chasing drug dealers around or working 24 hours straight. I also knew that I was facing mandatory retirement in seven years as DEA has a mandatory retirement age of 57. So, I needed to start thinking about retirement, maybe not for good but from the DEA, and how I could make myself more marketable. I also wanted to do something a little bit different. Although nothing stays the same and 25 years is a long time, the DEA only enforced one U.S. code, Title 21 – The Controlled Substances Act – so things really remained the same year after year. Sure, the drugs came and went, but the job was basically the same. And I wanted to mentor young agents and share my experiences with them in the hope that I could make them better agents. So, I put in for the promotion and I got it.

During my four years as a Group Supervisor, I had the opportunity to supervise a couple of pretty amazing investigations. One of them was the arrest and extradition of an individual in the United Kingdom who was sending out millions and millions of pills – ecstasy, tramadol, Molly (powder ecstasy), LSD, PCP, GHB, and a host of others – worldwide through the mail and accepting bitcoin as payment. The other one, and the most intriguing one, was an investigation that one of the TFOs in my office did in which he had a two-year wiretap investigation which focused on BlackBerry Messenger (BBM) intercepts.

33
Blackberry Messenger (BBM) Investigation

The TFO was Ryan Elsey and he was an absolute genius. He was a savant. Gifted! While he was in my group, he was actually recruited by DEA Headquarters to initiate this investigation. And the crazy part was none of the targets were in Ohio, or even in the U.S. They wanted him to use Title 21 U.S.C. Section 959, commonly referred to as "959" investigations. This is the importation code of Title 21. More about this later.

In this investigation, they first wanted Ryan to wiretap BlackBerry Messengers (BBMs) used by high level DTOs operating between Panama, Guatemala, Ecuador, Mexico, and Colombia. These groups specialized in using maritime vessels to smuggle multi-hundred-kilograms of cocaine from these countries into the U.S. They were a maritime smuggling operation. The BBMs were not the old direct connect phones that you're thinking about that had that annoying chirp and "alert" feature, but it was a BBM app on their cell phones on which they could use to message one another. That was what we were going to tap. I remember thinking how crazy it was that we were going to wiretap an app.... tap that app!!! LOL. But I had to remember that times had changed. Once when I was in Miami, I initiated a wiretap on a fax machine! So, who was I to judge?

The DTOs were transporting multi hundred-kilogram loads of cocaine using maritime vessels in the Caribbean Sea. When we asked DEA Headquarters which BBM targets and which DTOs we were supposed to target, DEA Headquarters said to leave that up to them. They would be the clearinghouse for intelligence information coming out of the DEA offices in Panama, Guatemala, Ecuador, Mexico, and Colombia. So, we had our targets. Kind of.

Let me say that a 959 investigation was kind of tricky, mainly the prosecution of 959 defendants. A 959 investigation dictated that the defendants in an investigation were charged in the first location, or judicial district in which they entered the U.S. If a smuggler was arrested off the coast of Miami with kilogram quantities of cocaine, for example, and he was brought to Miami to be booked, processed and jailed, then that would be the charging judicial district, the SDFL. So, in our investigation, if we were to arrest someone doing the same smuggling venture, and we wanted to charge him in the SDOH where Columbus is located, that defendant would have to be flown directly to Ohio. That was going to be a bit dicey for us going forward.

My supervisors at the time, Matt Heufelder and Mauricio (Mo) Jimenez, were all for it, especially Mo since he had come to the Columbus office by way of DEA Headquarters so he was a big DEA Headquarters proponent. Matt was a big picture guy and thought it would be great to put Columbus on the DEA map along with the other DEA big boys like New York, Miami, and Los Angeles. First, we had to get a prosecutor on board. I knew exactly who it had to be – Dave DeVillers, my old buddy from the SNP investigation. It was an obvious choice. And, when Ryan came to me asking about a prosecutor and I mentioned Dave's name, he asked if I would contact Dave and set up a meeting and then attend the meeting as well. Ryan stated that he would normally do it, but he didn't know Dave that well. I said that I would. No problem.

The funny thing that I remember about my phone call to Dave and the meeting was that as soon as I reached Dave on the phone and requested a meeting, he said that he would meet us but if it had to do with a new investigation, he was way too busy. He said he couldn't take on any more at the moment. I knew he was going to say this as the best prosecutors are always the busiest as they are few and far between. But I also knew Dave well. I knew how much he liked a challenge and do something that no one had done before. Well, at least in the SDOH.

So, we all met a few days after that phone call. Ryan, Dave, and me at Dave's office at the U.S. Attorney's Office in Columbus. We laid out the investigation to him. We told him about how DEA Headquarters would farm out leads to us that they had received from DEA offices in Guatemala, Panama, Ecuador, Colombia, and Mexico. We would then initiate BBM wiretaps on the members of the organization. And how, if anyone was arrested smuggling on the high seas, they would be prosecuted in the SDOH by way of the 959 section of Title 21. He loved it. He wanted in. I knew it! There was no way Dave was going to pass that up. It was too much of a challenge. It was a chance for Dave to do something in the SDOH that no other AUSA had done. So, we had our team. It was Ryan, Ryan's partner – a young, aggressive, and talented agent by the name of Tom Costanzo, Dave, and me.

It didn't take long for DEA Headquarters to pass us our first BBM number to wiretap. Ryan started the affidavit which was done within a few days. As I said, he was a genius. What I needed an Intelligence Analyst for over the years when I was writing affidavits, he could do himself. He could take piles of data, mainly phone records, and crunch the numbers himself. He didn't need any excel spreadsheets or other computer programs.

Here was the other scary thing. Remember, earlier when I mentioned the back-and-forth game with sending an affidavit to DOJ/Main Justice with all of the edits and corrections? Well, Ryan's affidavits would come back with zero corrections needed. **Zero.** In all my years of law enforcement, I had never seen that or heard of that.

The first lead given to us was targeting the Frank "El Gordo" Valone, maritime drug trafficking organization. Valone was Ecuadorian and ran his organization out of Ecuador. He was a maritime smuggler who would transport boatloads, no pun intended, of cocaine on behalf of drug trafficking organizations in

Colombia, Mexico, Panama, and Guatemala.

Ryan proceeded to write the affidavit and within a few days we were intercepting the BlackBerry messages. This was June, 2017. We intercepted the Valone organization for almost three months learning the names of other members of the organization, trafficking methods, maritime smuggling routes, and so forth. As always, we started slowly and methodically, and we built our puzzle, piece by piece. It was painstaking, arduous work, but it paid off at the end, as always. The one thing that took a while to get used to was that we were intercepting messages from an organization in Ecuador. There was no surveillance to conduct as we did not have any members of the organization in Ohio, or even in the U.S. for that matter.

We finally got our break in August of 2017. This group had been planning a smuggling venture for quite some time and now it had come to fruition. The load of cocaine had been delivered, and it was ready to be transported to the U.S. We had a **ton** of work to do to get ready to intercept this vessel. The most important was my daily conversations with JIATF South in Key West, Florida.

JIATF South stood for the Joint Interagency Task Force. It was situated at the Naval Air Station in Key West, Florida. The main function of this task force was to conduct detection and monitoring operations in their area of responsibility to interdict maritime smuggling vessels, as well as aircraft, that were believed to be involved in drug trafficking, and the DEA was a key component of JIATF.

Every day, sometimes two to three times a day, I would call JIATF and report the latest messenger intercepts while they scoured the Caribbean looking for suspect vessels. They would basically take the intelligence information that I had received from Ryan and relay it to the U.S. Coast Guard who was punching holes in the ocean looking for anything that stood out. Then it happened. The U.S. Coast Guard spotted a suspect vessel.

To better understand this BBM investigation, an article was

written about it. It explained that a judicially authorized wiretap investigation on a BlackBerry device led to a million-dollar cocaine seizure on the high seas. It went on to outline how four men raced a speedboat in the area of the Galapagos Islands with almost 1,600 pounds of cocaine on board as their cargo was intercepted by the U.S. Coast Guard cutter. A decision to launch a helicopter off the deck of their cutter was made, and then it was game on. Seeing the helicopter off in the distance, the speedboat attempted to outrun the helicopter, all while tossing duffle bag after duffle bag of cocaine over the side of the speedboat. The attempt to outrun the helicopter continued even as the helicopter fired warning shots in the area of the speedboat. When this failed and the speedboat continued with its escape plan, the helicopter decided to fire shots right into the speedboat's engines in an attempt to disable the boat. The boat was, indeed, disabled and four men on the speedboat were arrested. The U.S. Coast Guard then backtracked the escape route that the speedboat took and collected all of the duffle bags of cocaine. The four men on board the speedboat were charged and eventually transported to the U.S. where they were prosecuted.

In this same article, AUSA Dave DeVillers alluded to the fact that they (the DEA) wouldn't have had a prosecutable case without the BBM intercept as it was the only way that the speedboat could have been located, the cocaine seizure made, and the four individuals identified.[5]

That was an amazing seizure. Anytime we could take 1,590 pounds of cocaine off the street, or ocean in this case, was a really good feeling. But at the time, the celebration was short lived as we needed to focus on getting the four crew men and the cocaine back to Ohio. These were daunting tasks to say the least.

The first order of business was to get the defendants back to Ohio while respecting the 959 section of Title 21. We had to find a way to transport the prisoners all the way from Guantanamo Bay to Ohio (the U.S. Coast Guard makes it their practice to transport any defendants arrested on the Caribbean Sea to Guantanamo Bay until the charging district determines what to do with them).

But how were we going to get to Guantanamo Bay which is in Cuba? I then remembered something from my seven years in the Miami Field Division. I remembered the division's airwing capacities. They have a number of fixed wing aircraft and even helicopters that are used to support missions and investigations throughout Florida, as well as the Caribbean. I contacted the agent in charge of the Miami office Airwing Group requesting air support for a couple agents from my office to go from Florida to Guantanamo Bay.

They were great, just fantastic. They were excited about our seizure and eager to assist us. The plan was that we would fly a team of agents to Florida on commercial air. Tom Costanzo volunteered to lead the team. From there, the airwing would then fly the same two agents to Guantanamo Bay. They would have an aircraft big enough to hold the pilot, co-pilot, the two agents from my office, and the four defendants.

They would then depart Guantanamo Bay with the prisoners, but this time they would stop to re-fuel in the Bahamas. This way, the aircraft would be able to make it all the way to Columbus. Remember, the first location the defendants touched down in the U.S. is where they would be prosecuted as determined by the 959 protocol. If they had attempted to fly from Guantanamo Bay to Columbus, they wouldn't have had enough fuel to make it the entire way. They would have had to stop and re-fuel and wherever that was would have to be where the defendants were prosecuted, so that wouldn't work for prosecution in the SDOH. We had to get them to Columbus.

In the meantime, I also had to get two other important tasks completed – visas for the defendants and a pass-through letter for the ten kilograms of cocaine. It had been decided at that point that the kilograms that were seized would be transported by a U.S. Coast Guard cutter to San Diego, California which the U.S. Customs was using as sort of a repository, or collection point at the time for these types of cases and seizures. The U.S. Coast Guard instructed us that we would need to send an agent to San Diego to assist with the processing of these kilograms. Ryan made that trip while Tom assisted with the prisoner transport in Guantanamo Bay. We didn't need to worry about the cocaine for right now, except for the ten kilograms.

Many times, prosecutors would want a sample from a large seizure like this in case any of the defendants proceeded to trial. That way there would be a representative sample to show to the jury as evidence. In this case, we decided that ten kilograms of cocaine would be a proper representative sample. No prosecutor was going to demand that we maintain 1,590 kilograms of cocaine, but often they do want a sample. My God, can you imagine if they did? Where in the hell would you store it? In order to get the ten kilograms into the country, I needed to get a pass-through letter since we were basically importing it into the country ourselves with the four defendants. This was the same exact type of pass-through letter that I had explained a few different times before, no different. These are kind of pain to get, but I had gotten a few throughout my career, so I knew the process. After a few days, we had the letter. Now, I needed visas.

I found this strange. We had to get the four defendants visas to enter the country...to go to jail. Seriously. The Department of Homeland Security/Homeland Security Investigations (DHS/HSI) took any type of entry into the U.S. very seriously. So, I had to go through our headquarters who, in turn, would coordinate with DHS/HSI to get the four defendants their visas to enter the country. Basically, they would use the visas to enter the U.S. when they arrived in Columbus, and then they would be booked/processed and finally transported to jail. So, that was done.

Believe it or not, all of this went off without a hitch. Ryan traveled out to San Diego to assist with the processing of the 1,590 kilograms of cocaine. Tom traveled down to Guantanamo Bay with his team to assist with the transport of the four defendants from Cuba to the Bahamas to Columbus. He also took possession of the ten-kilogram cocaine representative sample from U.S. Customs while he was there. The Airwing was met by a team of agents when it touched down in Columbus. We had the four visas waiting so the defendants were processed into the U.S. without any issues. Then they were booked/processed and next transported to the Franklin County Jail where they would remain while their judicial proceedings took place.

Below is a photo of Mo with the Ohio State Highway Patrol waiting for the Airwing to arrive in Columbus.

Assistant Special Agent in Charge (ASAC) Mauricio Jimenez directs the Ohio State Patrol as to the route they will be taking once the DEA Airwing lands after flying from Guantanamo Bay, Cuba with the four defendants from the BBM investigation.

Ryan and Tom continued with this investigation, identifying, and arresting other members of this organization who were suppliers of the cocaine. They also went on to do a few more of these BBM investigations right up until BBM discontinued the use of their app. But that was the first BBM investigation that we did, and I'll never forget it.

DEA Task Force Officer Ryan Elsey (left) and DEA Special Agent Tom Costanzo (right) escort a member of the Francisco GOLON-Valenzuela Organization (center) from the DEA Aircraft after extraditing him from Bogota, Colombia.

34
Retirement

Coming into the year 2020, I had decided to retire at the end of the year, December 31st. It would be bittersweet, but it was time. By that time, I would have had 30 years with the DEA, and I had loved every minute. But I really wanted to do something new. I think it's very important in life to keep challenging and re-inventing ourselves. And after 30 years of basically doing the same thing every day, that wasn't happening.

Also, I feel that it's very crucial to the success of any organization to keep the managers and supervisors fresh and new. They should be rotated every few years. What I mean by that is if managers and supervisors take a spot and never leave until they are forced out, the organization gets stagnant. There aren't any new bodies or new ideas. Fresh blood is always good for an organization.

Plus, it's just not fair to others. I think it's important to give those behind us a chance to step up and supervise. It is what keeps an organization relevant. I could have stayed where I was until mandatory retirement at the age of 57. If I would have done that, I would have been in that supervisor's role for seven years. That's entirely too long, and it's not fair to DEA as an organization or to other, younger agents. No, four years was enough for me. I had enough of badges, bad guys & busts! It was someone else's turn!!

REFERENCES

1. "Former Medellin Cartel Associate Pleads Guilty To Drug Trafficking Conspiracy." www.dea.gov/press-releases, May 3, 2011, Former Medellin Cartel Associate Pleads Guilty To Drug Trafficking Conspiracy (dea.gov)

2. "Twenty-two Charged In Alleged Drug Trafficking Conspiracy." www.justice.gov/usao-sdoh, December 11, 2013, Twenty-two Charged In Alleged Drug Trafficking Conspiracy | USAO-SDOH | Department of Justice

3. Eric Lyttle. "Is this really the end of Columbus' most infamous gang?" *Columbus Monthly*. March 17, 2017.

4. Amber Hunt, Kevin Grasha, Liz Dufour, Madeline Mitchell. "Untouchable Attorney Charged with Human Trafficking." Originally published in the *Cincinnati Enquirer* on March 21, 2019. Republished in USA Today on October 24, 2020.

5. Thomas Brewster. "Exclusive: How a BlackBerry Wiretap Helped Crack a Multi-Million Dollar Cocaine Cartel." *Forbes Magazine*. October 25, 2019.

Made in the USA
Monee, IL
20 May 2021